A Paradise for the Poor

Hussar, Standard & Caroline, Alberta
Letters of Ole Nissen
1923 - 1937

edited by Joan Walter

Published by
Alberta Records Publication Board
Historical Society of Alberta
General Editors:
David W. Leonard and
David C. Jones
Vol. xiii

Canadian Cataloguing in Publication Data

Nissen, Ole, 1903-1979.
"A paradise for the poor"

(Historical Society of Alberta ; 13)
Includes bibliographical references and index.
ISBN 0-929123-11-5

1. Nissen, Ole, 1903-1979--Correspondence. 2. Danish Canadians--Alberta--Biography.* 3. Pioneers--Alberta--Correspondence. 4. Frontier and pioneer life--Alberta.
I. Walter, Joan, 1937- II. Alberta Records Publication Board. III. Historical Society of Alberta. IV. Title. V. Series: Historical Society of Alberta (Series) ; v. 13.
FC3700.D3Z7 2001 971.23'302'092 C00-911545-5
F1080.D3N57 2001

Front cover photo: Ole Nissen,1929
Back cover photo: Ole Nissen with Violin, 1938

First printing 2001

Printed and bound in Canada by Friesens Corporation,
Altona, Manitoba, R0G 0B0

Published by
Alberta Records Publication Board
Historical Society of Alberta

CONTENTS

DEDICATION

In memory of Ole (Helge) and Emily Nissen,
Herman and Isobel Petersen,
—and to Audrey Nissen,
with love and respect.

NOTES ON TRANSLATION, EDITING AND SOURCES

Finding and translating the material in this book was a gradual process. All of father's letters, and most of his diaries, were written in Danish. In 1973 he translated many of his letters and his main diary up to March 8, 1925, adding a few comments. In 1978 he retyped them, adding other notes, getting as far as February 9, 1924. He died in 1979, with the project unfinished. Other letters were found; two were translated by the Winnipeg Danish Consulate, the rest by my late cousin in Denmark, Ole Nissen. Recently, when I was looking for more material, my sister, Fay, loaned me father's large diary, in which there were 177 more pages, mostly in Danish, and two small diaries from father's childhood. Sonja Buhl translated these, along with a final letter from 1923, sent by my Danish cousin, Signe Esbjørn.

To ease the reading, I have introduced paragraphing, corrected father's spelling and punctuation, at times re-sequenced sentences, and re-phrased his wording.

Unless credited otherwise, all photos in this book are mine. Father's letters, a photocopied version of his diaries, my mother's diaries, and a number of the photos used herein, are held by the Archives of the Glenbow-Alberta Museum in Calgary.

Abbreviations:
GAA, Glenbow-Alberta Museum Archives
PAA, Provincial Archives of Alberta
PABC, Provincial Archives of British Columbia
VPL, Vancouver Public Library

ACKNOWLEDGMENTS

I owe my deepest gratitude to the late Alfred and Gudrun Nissen, father's brother and sister-in-law, for saving his letters and photos, and to their daughter, Signe Esbjørn of Denmark, for sending them to me, along with her own family photo. My cousin, Ole Nissen, also of Denmark, translated letters and passed along a priceless Danish heritage.

My manuscript, or excerpts, were read by Dr. Gary Enns of the history department of Assiniboine College, Manitoba; Fred McGuinness, writer and broadcaster; Dr. Gerald Friesen of the history department, University of Manitoba; and Dr. Rod Macleod, Alberta 2000 Centennial History Society. Thank you for comments and contacts.

While father had translated most of his letters and part of his diary, many more diary pages and another letter were later found. Sonja Buhl, an English teacher in Denmark before she emigrated to Winnipeg, skillfully translated these. Rheanne Smith of the Documentary Heritage Society of Alberta and Lindsay Moir and April Miller of the Archives of the Glenbow-Alberta Museum were valued guides. Gary Schang graciously shared photos and information about his father, Walter Schang, along with historical details. Our late friend, Dr. George Lammers, lent his archeological insight regarding the Alberta Wintering Hills. Dean Petersen helped with agricultural concerns, and Sharyl Mayer of the Winnipeg Commodity Exchange explained historic grain pricing. Also, my sincere thanks to Wade and Cathy Petersen, Edna Jones, Lillian (Harmer) Wilson and Lola (McKinney) Wall.

I relied heavily on the excellent history, The *Hussar Heritage*. Dianne Taubert, of the Hussar Historical Society carefully checked my manuscript for local historical accuracy and gave additional information. *The Grass Roots* of Dorothy also identified people father mentions.

I am grateful to the Alberta Records Publication Board for their encouragement and especially to Dr. David Jones, editor, for his interest before the manuscript was developed. Dr. David Leonard also helped in editing. Agricore awarded a grant to help with software and research.

Finally, I thank my friends and family for their assistance and feedback; and especially my husband, Art, for digitally restoring photos, providing graphics, and for his unstinting support in every way.

Joan Walter

INTRODUCTION

"Just about the first day I started here, I was asked to harness twelve horses in two teams, and then he [*the farmer*] took one team and I the other one. I have never driven a team with more than two horses, so you can imagine I had better be careful, and the first week after we had started in the fields I could not close my hands from holding onto those leather straps." —

Ole Nissen

The diaries, letters, and photos of Ole Nissen.

He was christened Helge Christian König Nissen, but his first name (pronounced Hel' yeh) sounded strange to Canadian ears, so he was first called "Chris," then "Ole." In correspondence with his family overseas, he remained "Helge."

Ole (Helge), my father, wrote the first paragraph above in 1923, just after emigrating to western Canada. As he lived and worked, mostly on the Alberta prairies, he kept a diary and wrote letters to his family in Denmark, telling of events as they happened, day by day, year by year, never knowing what was around the corner.

Father died in 1979, but left his writing, and it is this I would share—not because his story is so unique, but because it is a reflection of the times he lived in. Much of what happened in his life happened to others across the West. Father wrote about details—"riding the rods," complaints in the bunkhouses, games at country dances, confrontations with ornery horses and poor roads—and about wider issues—setting out to farm, the depressed economy, the drought, weeds and pestilence.

On first arriving in Alberta, father just wanted a well-paying job, and though unused to physical labour, he spoke English and was full of youthful enthusiasm. So whether it was working on a farm, in a restaurant, or at a railroad tie camp, it did not matter. But as time went on, he became lonely and disenchanted, wishing for something more permanent. He struck up a friendship with his employer, Walter Schang, a farmer and contractor north of Hussar, Alberta, and, partly through him, father embraced the prairie and its people. Like many settlers, father was caught in a wave of optimism, and though he still had much to learn about farming, he decided to try it himself, beginning in 1926.

Father's great-grandfather, Hans Olufsen, had been a farmer in Denmark during the terrible European depression in the early 1800s, augmenting his meagre income by playing at country dances. His son, Ole Hansen Nissen, became a schoolteacher, a church singer, a musician and a horticulturist, recording his life in an autobiography.

Father's father, Johannes Nissen—Ole Hansen's son—was also a schoolteacher and church singer at Paarup, Denmark, where the family lived. He was a talented musician and a horticulturist, spending untold hours cross-breeding to improve the quality of flowers, produce and trees in his extensive gardens and orchard. He wrote many letters and kept a running diary. He was a linguist and a leader in the community. He and his wife, Signe (father's mother), were devoted to each other and played music with my uncle Alfred, forming a trio—Signe on piano, Johannes on cello, and Alfred on violin. The family home, next to the gardens and orchard, was attached to the school, the buildings of which formed a square, with a good sized yard in the middle.

It was here, in 1903, that father was born, an "afterthought" with five grown siblings.

When he was about five years old, father's parents began teaching him the piano, but he decided to learn violin, like his father,

The Nissen family. Ole's parents: at piano, Signe; with cello, Johannes. Ole's siblings: seated, left, Ingrid; with violin, Alfred. Far right: Johannes Jr. and Gudrun (Alfred's wife). Paarup, Denmark, c 1913. Photo digitally restored.

and was given a three-quarter size instrument with which to begin. Of his childhood, father wrote, "There is no doubt that I was badly spoiled, and allowed to amuse myself as best I could." Yet why he was discouraged from playing on neighbouring farms, he did not know, but suspected his parents may have been somewhat class-conscious.

In 1915, at age eleven, father lost both of his parents. First his mother fell ill, and, as she lay dying of uterine cancer, he began to keep a daily diary, describing in detail the events of her passing. Four months later, his father died after an operation for cancer and a stomach perforation.

From then on, father was lovingly but strictly raised and guided by his brother, Alfred, and his wife, Gudrun, who had their own three daughters. They lived at the harbour city of Nykøbing, Falster, where Alfred was teacher and principal of his privately owned school. Father's notes describe a happy life with Alfred and Gudrun: trying hard at school, caring about his grades, participating in school events, even organizing a collection for teachers' Christmas presents. His lessons included English, French and German, and his grade average in 1918 was 5.46 out of a possible 6.

Ole Nissen and siblings. Standing, l to r: Vilhelm, Alfred, Johannes Jr., and Eijner. In front: Lex, Ole, and Ingrid. Photo taken at their home the day of their father's—Johannes's—death. Denmark, 1915.

Ole's Brother and sister-in-law—also, foster parents—Alfred and Gudrun Nissen, and their daughters, Signe, Tove and Grethe. Denmark, 1922.

The First World War, raging at this time, seems to have hardly touched him at all. In his little notebook diary, he wrote of skating, books, music, and Charlie Chaplin movies. He described birthday parties (mentioning the goodies first in his list of presents), dancing lessons, which he especially enjoyed—including folk dancing and the mazurka, and sailing out into the harbour in a small boat, then having to row back. He told of accidents such as breaking a window and having to order a new one, spilling ink on the carpet and having to remove the stain, and of having to keep a financial account, which Alfred reviewed.

He would tell us later that, if he had not learned his violin lessons, he was made to cut a switch from a tree, with which he was punished—birch was worst. He also had to go for walks with Alfred, for reasons he did not understand at the time. Only as an adult did he realize that their discussions had been a time of valuable intimacy.

In 1919, when his formal education was ending at grade 10, father bought a diary in which he would record events for the next twenty years. He was now sixteen, and it was time for him to choose a career. His five siblings were already established: Vilhelm, the eldest, was a sailor, soon to be first mate; Eijner was a chartered accountant; Alfred, of course, a teacher; Ingrid, a home-maker, married to a musician; Johannes, a blacksmith; and Alexander (Lex), a department store manager in England.

Ole (Helge) Nissen, age sixteen, Nyborg, Denmark, 1919.

Father decided to become a station agent with the Danish State Railways, eventually moving to Nyborg where his married brother, Vilhelm, lived, and with whom he was very close. About then, he began writing to Alfred and Gudrun, at first enthusiastically describing his duties:

selling tickets and parcel postage, counting cash, learning about the telegraph and Morse code, and so on. His wage of 100 krone, out of which came 78 for room and board, seemed small but adequate. Augmenting this was a stipend from Alfred, for which he had to account. Six months into his training, he wrote exams, coming out first in his class. He then became a tested traffic-apprentice with evening and night duty.

For the next two and a half years, names and themes appear in his diary that would be echoed later in Canada. First, there was Clara, an attractive young woman, introduced to him at Vilhelm's. They occasionally visited and corresponded for two years, when, one day in 1920, she broke off the relationship. Other women are mentioned in his diary, a line or two here and there, but he wrote three pages about Clara (under the heading: Clara Roed), passionately turning fact into obvious fiction, then giving up, adding that he had been transferred, and had grown tired of her. But the suspicion is that he was quite hurt. Their relationship would strike up again, briefly, in years to come, and he would mention to me, wistfully, about a woman in Denmark he had deeply cared for.

By January 1921, father, now eighteen, was having serious money problems. A curious letter was then written on the sly by Maren Johanne, his godmother at Paarup, whom he had come to visit. She loved father, but took her responsibilities seriously, writing her concerns to Alfred:

> He is sitting [*here*] playing his violin. He has just told me that last night he joined a dancing class, and I asked him what he wore on his feet. "The boots I'm wearing," he said, referring to a pair of brown boots which have never been repaired, and which have no soles underneath except for rags, so they were quite wet inside.

When she advised father to ask Alfred for boot repair money, he refused. Maren feared that father would no longer listen to anyone, and suggested that Alfred order him home and straighten him out. Father came home, and the issue was resolved.

From his own perspective, father was doing both well and badly—well, because he had passed another exam and was now an assistant traffic agent, unusual for one so young. All were happy and pleased with him, and he had close friends. One of these was an apprentice, Mortensen. Both of them visited the sociable family of a merchant and implement dealer whom father did his best to impress and was invited back often. To his delight, one of the four daughters played duets with him, she on piano, father on violin—semi-classical music such as "Angel's Serenade," "Traumeri," and "Evening Chimes."

But he was also in debt. He had little will power, and Mortensen had even less. Too often they played chess. They also played cards for money, which he was finished with, father told Alfred.

> I don't understand how to keep my money. I get paid 165 kr. (it's greatly reduced because I'm at a country station). For board and room: 110 kr. Taxes: that came quite unexpected—45 kr. Left then is 10 kr. which is gone for a pair of glasses that I got last month. I owe the tailor 10 kr. and Mortensen 30 kr. I can't go on "making do," especially with clothes, so I don't know what to do. I think that I badly need money, or else I don't know how I will manage. You wrote that you had decided to stop giving good advice and reproaches, but please, on the contrary, give me some pick-me-ups; it's helping all right.

The next year, 1922, father appealed to his brother, Lex, in England, for work in his store. Lex was now earning 20,000 kr. [*$4420 Cdn.*] a year, plus a percentage of the profit. But he was an exception, as Britain was still in the post-war depression. Lex replied:

> I am not surprised to hear that you have grown tired of the railways. One month was all I would care for. In regards to taking you in here I can only say that it is against the company regulations for a manager to engage his own brother or any of his family, and you have no idea whether you would be happier here; the beginning is hard, and later the responsibilities are great. My advice for you is to wait until next year. In the meantime, learn as much of the language as you can, and I will do everything I can to help you in the beginning. You have to remember that there are 1,190,000 people out of work here in England, and many would be happy with your job until times are better.

For the next six months, father worked, socialized with friends, dated often, and travelled around the country. But something crucial was missing. That fall, he visited Vilhelm, and, after a serious discussion, resolved to emigrate. Railways may have seemed exciting when he was young, but they offered little scope for an adventurous youth. Wages were small, and he was forever short of money. In England, the job situation was not improving. Around him, on train station walls, posters beckoned, extolling the virtues of Canadian farm life, and proclaiming opportunities for western immigrants. He was intrigued and eager to travel. More importantly, father had become increasingly dissatisfied with himself and his lifestyle. In Canada he wanted to turn over a new leaf.

The Wintering Hills, north of Hussar, 1989.

Like most newcomers, father knew little of southern Alberta, its past or present. The region circling his destination—Hussar, sixty miles east of Calgary—had a long history that would greet him at every turn. It was part of the North American Great Plains, flat as a table top except for a rippling band of hills, south of the confluence of the Rosebud and Red Deer Rivers, that had been sculpted by glaciers and glacial streams, depositing more recent sedimentation in the valleys. They were known as the Wintering Hills, where father would live, work and play for dances. His livestock would feed on the diminishing sea of prairie wool where thousands of buffalo had grazed for centuries. In his fields, he would find their bleached skulls, and arrowheads left by the Blackfoot who had fed on the buffalo and traded with the Europeans from the mid-1700s until the 1870s. The Hills then became the winter quarters of Métis, who sought water, shelter and grazing.

Ranch leases dated from the 1880s, but, as pressure for agricultural lands intensified after 1900, the ranchers reluctantly yielded to sodbusters. In 1906 the Canadian Pacific Railway established the Western Section of its irrigation blocks—centred at Strathmore, extending south to Gleichen and east around Standard. Answering an aggressive sales campaign in the United States and eastern Canada, settlers raced in from 1908 to 1913. After buying irrigation land at Standard, in December 1909, an exuberant relative wrote my mother's parents, the Petersens, then in Nebraska—"I am doing well up here, and I have found a Paradise for the Poor."

The Reeves steam engine with which Walter Schang broke land for many early Hussar settlers. Probably coal-fueled here, it also burned wood and straw. With its own unique sound, it pulled 12-bottomed plows and large cultivators, tearing up the land quickly. c 1919. —Courtesy, Gary Schang.

Further east, a German syndicate purchased a large tract of twenty sections, and the name Huzzar—now anglicized—perhaps came from the German army officers involved.

The railroad reached Hussar in 1911, the hamlet grew in 1912, and more immigrants arrived in 1918 and 1919, mainly from the United States. They came from all walks of life—bank cashiers, high school teachers, loggers, miners, contractors, doctors, lawyers, engineers, but mostly dryland farmers. When father detrained at Hussar in 1923, there was a school, a restaurant, a hotel, a Masonic Lodge, two or more stores (one with a post office), three elevators, a lumberyard, one or two liveries, and a blacksmith shop.

The region was arid, and most of it was beyond the Western

Section of the CPR irrigation system (and ironically, where there was irrigation, settlers neither needed it as much, nor for decades did they use it much).[1] When father arrived, he was unaware that contract holders for CPR land and water had been fighting the railway for years, first over the erroneous classification of land on ridges, in bogs, and under water as irrigable. No sooner had farmers forced the railway to reclassify such land, than the post-war depression hit, and now, stressed to the limit, they could not honour even the adjusted contracts. In revolt, they threatened to leave en masse for Bolivia! On arrival, Father was also unaware that the vast agrarian empire to the east was disintegrating in drought and that farm abandonments were mounting by the hundreds. Dead Horse Lake, near Hussar, still held water, but, by 1929, it would be baked dry, and swirling alkali dust devils would rise in it night and day—a portent of what lay in store for my father.

Joan Walter with David C. Jones

---

[1] David C. Jones, *Feasting on Misfortune—Journeys of the Human Spirit in Alberta's Past* (Edmonton: University of Alberta Press, 1998), p. 80, ch. 7, 8. For the dryland disaster east of Hussar, see Jones, *Empire of Dust—Settling and Abandoning the Prairie Dry Belt* (Edmonton: University of Alberta Press, 1987).

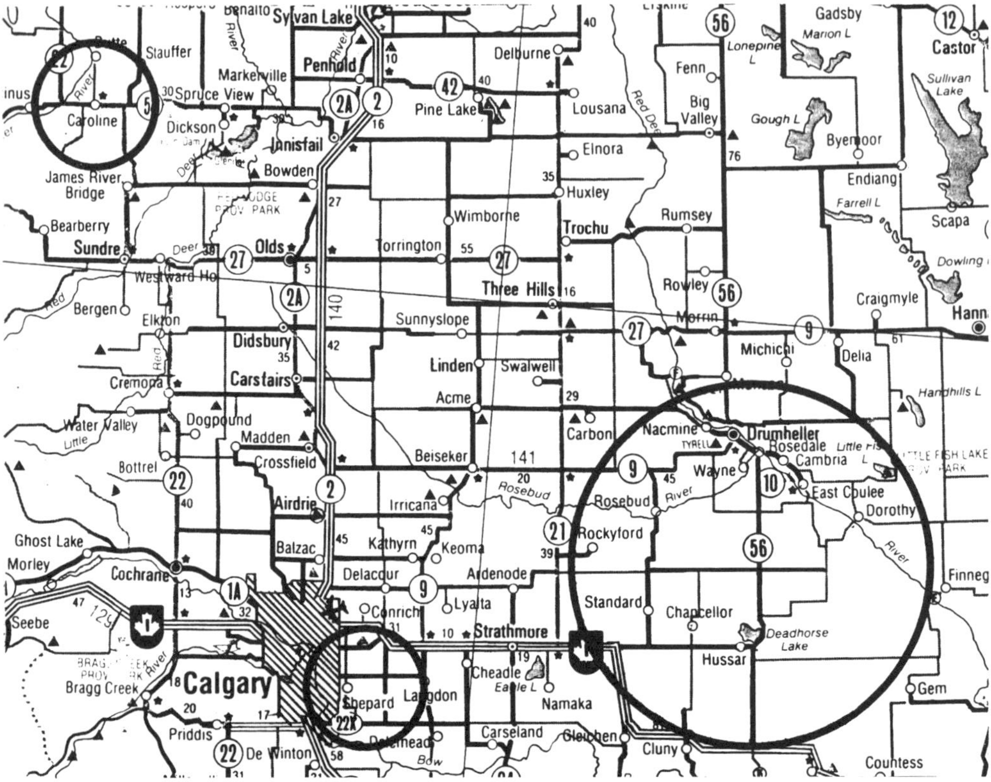

Southern Alberta, relevant areas circled. —Courtesy, Clear-view Maps, Ltd.

"I Was Pretty Much Of A Greenhorn" 1923 - 1926

"A picture of my companion and me in work clothes—April 2, 1923."
Ole Nissen, left, and Axel Madsen at Theodore Larsen's farm, Hussar, Alberta.

1923

By 1923, the area southeast and northeast of Hussar had been suffering from a long drought, beginning in 1917. Partly in response to the crisis, a new farm government was elected in Alberta in 1921. The Drought Area Relief Act of 1922 led to the Debt Adjustment Act of 1923, and the problems of debt would weigh heavily on the province for most of the next two decades. The price of wheat dropped in October 1923, and would stay down for the next seven months. As these events were unfolding, father arrived in Hussar, worked as a farm labourer, then headed west to British Columbia.

Hussar, April ?, 1923
Dear Gudrun and Alfred!

Well now, I have arrived here all right. I thank you so many times for the money. It was, of course, more than adequate, and I still have $35 after having bought work clothes, etc. I did not have time to talk to the treasurer of the school fund in Odense, but he got the receipt.

The journey went well. Vilhelm accompanied me to Esbjerg as you know. The voyage across the North Sea was fine. Of course, there were a number of seasick people, but I was not sick. There were quite a few Danes, and I slept with three. On March 15, we arrived in England at 5 p.m. Here in Harwich we were checked by a doctor, and our passports were looked at. At 6 p.m. the train left for London, and you bet it went fast. At 8:30 we were in London, where some agents put us into some big buses; that was all we got from that automobile trip, an hour's drive from one station to another. When we arrived at the other station, we stood there waiting until 11:30 when the train left for Liverpool.

We arrived there at 4 o'clock in the morning, and we had to wait there until the steamer left on the 17th in the morning. There is not much to talk about my impression of England. The bit of time I could see the landscape while going from Harwich, it was like Denmark, and I have nothing to tell about Liverpool through which I walked a full day. It was a very damp and quite dirty city.

On the 17th in the morning, we sailed from there. It was, as promised, in a big steamer I crossed the Atlantic. I guess I could tell you quite a bit about it, but I'll leave it at that. Once in a while, there were big waves and lots of seasick people, so I almost fancy myself a good sailor. We saw neither icebergs nor anything else interesting in the sea. On the 25th we arrived in Halifax and went through quite an ordeal which lasted for four hours. It was rather a cold impression I got of the new country: ice and snow all over.

Well! We arrived at 3 in the afternoon and left at 9 o'clock in the evening. The Canadian trains have large, comfortable cars: the seats can recline so you can lie down and sleep excellently, and above there is a row of large drawers which you can pull out so two people can lie down and sleep in them. Well now, you will have to excuse me for I have not had any time to write for all of two weeks, so I believe I will have to ask you to get the letter I have written Vilhelm for I must admit that regarding time here I have miscalculated. There is not a free moment neither Sundays nor holidays; well today, Sunday, there are two hours, but more about that later.

I travelled with a young man who was going to Hussar, a small town near Standard, so we went together. During the journey, we talked about our near future, and he told me that he was going to his sister and brother-in-law who were going to get him a job with a Canadian, and when I told him that I was going to see a man whom I did not know, who was Danish and who maybe already had men enough, he said that I should go with him, and that was what I did. But about all this I hope you can learn through my letter to Vilhelm. I am working for an American on an 840 acre farm. His name is Moffat.[2] Right now we are only two on the farm, but in two weeks his wife and children, ten and eight years old, are coming out here. Just about the first day I started here, I was asked to harness twelve horses in two teams, and then he took one team and I, the other one. I have never driven a team with more than two horses, so you can imagine I had better be careful, and the first week after we had started in the fields I could not close my hands from holding onto those leather straps. Of course, it will have to be farming on a large scale when two people will have to look after an 840 acre farm, and so it is. All machinery is much bigger than at home.

But now I shall tell you about my day. We get up at 4 - 4:15 or 4:30, usually at 4 o'clock. Then I go out into the pasture to look for the horses; well, I don't walk, I take the riding horse which is

---

[2] Charlie Moffat, likely known also as Denton Moffat, arrived in the Hussar area with his family from Paradise, Montana, in 1918. CPR literature had led them to believe that they could make a fortune in Alberta and return to the United States in a few years. Denton died at an early age, with his son, Johnny taking over the farm.

always at home in the stables, but then I ride out to find the horses (the horses are *always* outside at night—also in the winter). It usually takes me half an hour. When I have them back home, I am awake. Then I feed them hay. Then I feed fourteen hogs (they all have young ones; Moffat has forty more, but they are loose on the prairie, and I only see them when I am out in the fields). The hogs get ground wheat and water. I have to walk the distance from Maraviglia to the school [*at home in Denmark*] about fourteen times with two buckets of water. When I have fed the hogs, I have to help a little lamb we have because the ewe will not let it suckle. First I will have to catch the ewe and push it over and then hold it down. After that, the horses get ground oats. We have only fourteen work horses here; where the others are I do not know, but the farmers brand their animals (horses as well as cattle) and send them out onto the prairie. All this feeding must only take two hours. At 6 o'clock we eat breakfast. In the beginning, I could not make it, but now I am doing better.

After breakfast I leave for the stable to groom all the horses and harness as many as I can, usually only my own six before Moffat arrives. At 7:30 we are on our way, and then we sow and harrow. He has 300 acres of land for wheat, and those we already have behind us now, and then we are going to sow another 100 acres of wheat. I am harrowing—I have four harrows and a small seat on which I can sit. There is a lot to look after, believe you me. But I learn very quickly all this work, and that is because Moffat does not stand there explaining for half an hour; no! here you are, there are the horses and the tools, and there is the land you have to work.

At 12 o'clock we go home for "dinner." At 1 o'clock in the field again and at 5:30 - 6 o'clock home again. Then he goes in to prepare "supper" while I feed the horses and the hogs, like I do in the morning. When I have finished that (usually at 7:30), we eat, and then we let the horses out, and then there is always something to do for about an hour. Then I am free but also so dead tired that I am in bed right away (9 o'clock).

The last hour in the evening I have mostly worked with the seed, shovelled it up into a wagon and then mixed with a mixture of blue vitriol [*probably copper sulfate, used to kill surface borne fungi*]. One evening we slaughtered a pig (it only took an hour because blood and *all* entrails were discarded). Another evening I hauled a dead horse, pig, and cow out onto the prairie; they had died during the winter and stank badly. Practically all cows and pigs are missing most of their ears because of frostbite.

There is not much difference between Sundays and weekdays here. Well! the food is better on Sundays; he takes more trouble preparing it then. Incidentally, he can cook well, that Moffat. For "breakfast": first porridge, then two fried eggs with some bacon and toast, and we drink coffee with it right from the porridge [*serving*] until we finish. For "dinner" we get some roasted meat and potatoes, no gravy but lots of raw onions and on top of it all two boiled eggs poured over it like gravy; after that, pie and cake; tea right from the beginning to the end. "Supper" is almost like "dinner." We eat bread with all meals.

The climate has already affected me very much. The sun burns, my whole face has peeled completely, and it hurts terribly when I shave. Now I have got something to rub into my skin. One Sunday I had a little time to myself and I ought to have written, but Moffat told me I could take the riding horse and go over to the Larsens', and that was what I did.[3] To comfort me, they told me that I could look forward to when we had finished seeding, because then we would not work so hard. Mrs. Larsen's brother has started to work on a large farm of approximately six sections = 3840 acres. He was at Larsens' the day I visited them. He could not understand a bit of anything they said to him, but it was all right anyhow. The landscape here is hill after hill, only prairie, but we live right next to "Dead Horse Lake," a dirty salt lake about the size of a section. I still have not really had the opportunity to examine the flora and fauna here, but I hope I will later. Well! We have gophers now and crocuses in large numbers. Moffat says that a gopher now in spring is the same as $5 [*lost*]. He has two dogs who every day snap a lot of them; they (the gophers) eat the grain we seed. Well, Alfred probably knows what they look like, but I would almost compare their size to that of a stoat [*weasel*]. Now you will ask if I miss Denmark, and I will have to answer no, not yet. I do not have the time. Well, I have started singing patriotic songs and do not think the revue hits I know are very good any more.

---

3 Theodore Larsen, emigrating from Denmark to the USA in 1915, had heard of Alberta prospects while attending a Danish "Folk High School" in Wisconsin. The next year, with a partner, he came to Hussar, farmed, and married a young Danish woman in 1922. Later, they sold the farm and moved north to Viking, farming until retirement.

Well! I will have to excuse myself for now. I do not have any more time but send my best regards and thanks for starting me off.

Lots of love to the children and yourselves from Helge

P.S. Would you please tell Mrs. Christensen a bit of this and ask her to give my regards to the whole family. I cannot write to them. If you want to write me, write to Helge Nissen, c/o Moffat, Box 86, Hussar, Alta.

[*Diary*:] Hussar, Alta. July 19th, 1923. Originally I had intended to start this diary from the time I left Denmark, but I did not find time to get started. On March 14 this year, I left Denmark. Everything went well on the trip. I went via Liverpool, Halifax, Montreal, Toronto, Regina, Bassano, to Hussar, Alberta. My fare cost me Kr. 840.00 [*Danish currency*]. There was a lot of snow in eastern Canada, but out on the prairie it was all gone. With the help of Mr. Clifgard, a Hussar storekeeper, I soon landed a job, working on the farm of Charley Moffat, an American.[4]

My first job was to harrow his fields, using 6 horses. Later I plowed with a sulky plow using 5 horses, 3 horses ahead and 2 horses behind them. Next I went discing with 8 horses, 4 and 4. I finished discing summerfallow last week, and tomorrow I'll have it all harrowed. Yesterday and today we hauled hay. The weather is very hot, 25° Celsius in the shade. We have had lots of rain, and the harvest will certainly be good this year. Moffat has more than 320 acres of crop out of which 20 acres are barley and 30 acres are oats. We are going to harvest the barley in two weeks. The land here is prairie all over, hill after hill; you cannot see far because of them. There is not much animal life here, just gophers, badgers, coyotes, and antelope.

I am hired for $30 a month for the first months and $40 for the last month of harvest. Moffat wants to hire Indians to stook his grain, and then I will have to change teams and do chores, but in a couple of weeks I shall clear out.[5] My first job was to harrow his fields, using 6 horses, 3 horses ahead and 2 horses behind them.

[4] Andrew Clifgard and family arrived in Hussar in 1914, from Wisconsin—first farming, then buying a grocery store in Hussar, where they also operated a post office and later a telephone exchange. This store burned down in 1920, as did his second in 1932, when the family moved away. Clifgard was mayor for five years, helpful to immigrants and very active in the community, as was his wife.

[5] Moffat would probably have hired the Blackfoot from the Gleichen reserve to thresh his grain.

On Sundays Mr. Moffat let me take his saddle horse and ride a couple of miles to visit with Axel and his folks. (That was the only opportunity I had to use my own language). Next, I went discing with 8 horses, 4 and 4. I finished discing summerfallow last week, and tomorrow I'll have it all harrowed. Yesterday and today we hauled hay. The weather is very hot. We have had lots of showers and have prospects for a real big harvest.

[*Added by father, 1978*:] I was breaking sod of prairie wool, and I can still remember the spills I took when the plowshare hit a big rock. The plow would fly out of the ground, dumping me out from my seat, often hitting the plow frame of the wheel. (As luck would have it, the horses were only too glad to stop when that happened). A few other incidents from this period still stand out in my mind—such as my first encounter with a swarm of flying ants! I had just finished pitching a big load of hay and was on my way to the haystack, tired, half asleep with no worries when they hit me on top of the load of hay. I had never had a like experience before, didn't know what to do. Sweating profusely, I could feel the ants crawling down my neck. The horses were also bothered and fighting the ants. I lost the lines, the horses took off at a run, and it wasn't long before the hayrack upset, and all the hay spilled all over the ground. Of course, I received a good bawling-out and was taught what to do in a similar case in the future.[6]

[*Diary*:] Sun., July 21, 1923. Today I received the camera I had ordered from Eatons. I visited with Axel and relatives, T. Larsens, and took four pictures.

Mon., July 22, 1923. I hauled hay this morning and went discing in the afternoon. This evening Moffat took me with him to visit Mr. Williams.[7] On the way back he asked me if I would work for him during the winter for $30 a month.

---

6 Another incident from this time father related to my brother, Eric: Father had been regularly milking a cow which had become quite a pet. One day, before driving off, the farmer ordered father to kill her and ready her for butchering. As there was no gun, or it was unavailable, father decided to use a hard blow to the head with the blunt side of an axe. But he was so upset that he brought down the axe on the wrong side, imbedding the blade in the cow's skull, where it stuck. The cow stood there, shaking her head from side to side, but the axe remained. Only with the greatest difficulty could father dislodge the axe and kill the poor beast.

7 Alonzo and Mabel Williams and family—hoping the arid conditions would improve Mabel's health—came from Washington in 1918. They farmed five miles northeast of Hussar.

Sun., July 28, 1923. I was at Larsen's. Before I left, I talked to him about how much I should get in wages for the harvest, and he took great offense and said that I should not have asked for more and I had to be crazy because I was only going to do chores for him during harvest.

Sun., August 4, 1923. We started to cut barley last Friday. Was at Hoeghts' today (who are also Danes, and live in Hussar).[8] They said I was a big fool to work for those wages at Moffat's. He said I could come to their place whichever day I wanted and get 40 cents per acre to stook his grain, and then I could get his job at a threshing machine, $5-6 per day.[9]

Later his uncle from Tudor [*a small village near Rockyford*] came. We had a nice time. When they were ready to leave for home, the uncle said that I could come over to his place and continue stooking, and then I could drive bundles and get $5-6 per day, and in case of rain, I could work with disc and harrow, so I did not need to lie idle and not get paid. During the winter, I could work for board if I wanted to. I only had to drive the children to school and help with chores. I almost took the job at once. Walked home in pitch darkness (three miles).

[*Aug. 5*], 1923. In the morning, I seeded barley, in the afternoon the same. In the evening, I took the first chance to explain to Moffat that I wanted to quit. As expected, he got very annoyed but said that, naturally, I had been convinced by that "Hoeght-kid," [*Louis*], but I had to take the consequences myself. Then he said that I had to give him time to find another man. I wanted to leave the next Friday, and he tore into the house swearing and later rushed to town in his car. I am wondering how this week will pass. On Saturday there will be a stampede in Hussar, and I would like to see it. I am not much of a man to say good-bye to a farmer. [*While translating, father replaced the last sentence with: "I don't like to have him mad at me"*].

October 7, 1923. I have neglected this diary again! Moffat & I came to an agreement. The harvest came; I did the chores. When Moffat's

---

[8] Born in Denmark, Raymond Hoeght emigrated at age fourteen with relatives to Nebraska in 1914, then to Rockyford in 1918. In 1920 he brought from Denmark his mother, sister and brother, Louis, with whom father played at dances. In 1921 Raymond bought a farm near town where father was offered harvest work.

[9] In the Standard-Hussar area, and perhaps across the prairies, "threshing" was generally pronounced "thrash'ing"; "granary" was "grain' ry"; and coyote was "kie' yoot"; and "chaps" were "shaps."

grain was cut, I took his binder and cut grain for Bob Halsey.[10] I received $4 a day for 14½ days. As soon as his crop was cut, Bob took his threshing machine over to Moffat. I hauled grain while Moffat's was threshed. When that was done, I went back with Bob, and hauled bundles for him at $5 a day. When I settled with Moffat, I received $160.

[*Added by father, 1978*:] The threshing crew slept in tents. We ate in a cook car that also followed the machine. On Sundays and wet days, we passed the time as best we could. Some of the men had discovered that I packed a violin with me, and on one occasion they asked me to play a tune. Having learned only semi-classical music in Denmark, I did my best to entertain them and put my heart and soul into it. However, I had their attention for only about three minutes, then they started to talk, and the louder I played, the louder they talked. They didn't even notice when I put my violin back in its case. I was very discouraged to say the least!

Autumn, 1923. I threshed with Bob Halsey for 1½ months and earned $150. After that I travelled to British Columbia. On the way I was cheated out of $15, being too much of a trusting soul. I had been threshing with a couple of old fellows, 40 - 45 years old. With threshing over, they suggested that I go with them to BC as there would be no more work on the prairies. I agreed, and we went to Bassano by car. We arrived there early in the evening. I took in a picture show. When I located them after the show, they were half drunk. We went to a hotel where they kept drinking. They wanted me to join them, but I refused; I can't drink that straight whisky. I took just a couple of sips and went to bed. Later on in the night, one of them woke me up and told me that he owed $15 to somebody and that he would pay me back as soon as we got to Calgary. I gave him the money mostly to get rid of him.

The train left at 4 a.m., and I had an awful time to wake them up and get them on the train. When we arrived at Calgary, they were still drunk. The first thing we did was to get a room at Hotel "Regis." I went to my room to get some more sleep; they said they would go for a walk first. When I woke up, there was no sign of them. When they did not show up the rest of the day, I knew darned

[10] Robert and Effie Halsey and four children, arrived from Creston, Washington, in 1918, leasing a section in the Wintering Hills, eighteen miles northeast of Hussar.

well that I could forget about my $15. I then took the first train to BC. In Calgary I had heard of a town called Cranbrook where there was lots of work available, so I bought a ticket to Cranbrook ($10).

I arrived there the next forenoon. I found the Employment Office without much trouble and got a job without much difficulty, working for a road building outfit at Bull River. I stayed with that job for three weeks. The scenery around there is great with lots of wild game. When I arrived at the camp, around dinner time, I looked for the foreman. When I found him, he stuck an axe in my hand and told me to follow him. We walked for about an hour before we came to the place of work. There were four other men working, and I was told to cut brush for a road through the most awful wilderness I've ever seen. I went at it with abandon, and soon got the sharp axe full of nicks. We quit work at 5 p.m. and walked back to the camp. The trail was on a mountainside, awful steep in places. The other four men were, of course, used to it and laughed at me when I was dead tired halfway home to camp.

After I had worked for a week, I got a lot tougher and didn't go at it so hard. After a few weeks, I was transferred to another shift that used grubaxe, pick & shovel to level the road making it fit to travel on. When the road was finally completed, I was told that there would be no more day-labour. From now on it would all be piecework, cutting RR ties. As I had no training in that kind of work, I told the foreman that I did not want to sign any contract binding me to something I knew nothing about. He kept me for a few more days, swamping, trimming branches and clearing trails for logs to be pulled out with a horse. The last day I was working, the foreman was particularly cranky; he said we were lazy. I got mad and warned him that if he did any more complaining, I would quit. He started to swear at me, and I threw the axe down, right in front of him (Canadian style) and went back to the camp.

There I became acquainted with a man whose name was Crawford. He decided to quit with me, and we decided to go to Vancouver where we would rent a cheap housekeeping room, do our own cooking and live cheaply. He had only $50, but I had $200, so he assured me that we would get along fine. I wanted to buy us RR tickets, but he insisted that there was a much better way to travel. Well, I was pretty much of a "Greenhorn," and he seemed to know a lot, so I agreed to his idea. We bought a ticket from Bull River to Cranbrook.

Bull River to Vancouver. Here we had lots of preparations to make. We sent the most of our possessions ahead by freight to Vancouver, keeping only a few blankets, the odd change of shirts, soap, towels and shaving kits. It turned out that Crawford had quite a few debts in Cranbrook, and by the time they were all paid up, he had only $5 left, and I had only $10, as I would not risk travelling with $200 in my pockets. We were therefore forced to stay at Cranbrook until Monday, so I could put my money in the bank. We left Monday afternoon, riding the freight. We spied a RR policeman walking up and down the track by the boxcars, so there was no chance to get on the train until it started to move. We walked up the line for a half mile. The locomotive gave a couple of whistles and started to move. Fortunately it was uphill at the start, so it did not gain speed very fast. We waited until an empty boxcar came along which already had ten other bums on it, and we rode it all the way to the town of Yahk. In Yahk I bought our supper, and then we walked back to the RR yard. Yahk is a border town between Canada and USA, and therefore some of the trains went to the U.S. and others to Kootenay Landing. When a train started toward Kootenay Landing, we were ready. The only car that would be any use to us was an open coal car, loaded nearly to top of the walls.

We hopped onto that car, happy to be on the move again. But after five minutes the train stopped, and we could hear that they were uncoupling the engine. We were just going to jump off when we heard someone walking by our car. Luckily he did not hear us, and eventually walked on. Crawford jumped off to find out what the situation was. After awhile I heard someone coming, and thinking it was him, I was about to ask what he had found out, when I discovered that it was the man from before. I flopped down on the coal and kept still as a mouse. After some five minutes, he walked away. I kept watching him and thought he was coming back, but this time it was Crawford. He had discovered nothing, but thought it best that we walk back to town as it appeared we were sitting on a side track and the rest of the train had left us. I did not want to go and suggested that we wait another fifteen minutes, as I had the idea that the engine could not pull the whole train up the steep hill, and maybe they would come back for the second half. He said O.K., and sure enough, five minutes later, the train came back. They coupled up to our section, and away we went to Kootenay Landing.

Ole Nissen, British Columbia, 1924.

Arriving there, we jumped off, and after awhile we found out that in order to go on, we would have to go three miles to the ferry and buy tickets for the ferry crossing Kootenay Lake. Walking, we finally reached Kootenay at 2 a.m., and we went to sleep in the depot. Next morning we walked down to the Landing, arriving at 11 a.m. The scenery on the way was magnificent, with mountains, waterfalls & mountain springs. About 10 a.m. we crossed a bridge over a river. It did not appear to be so long when first we saw it, but it took us half an hour to cross it. If a train had come along, we would have been in an awful fix! There was no way to get out of the way. At the Landing, we found a passenger ferry and a scow equipped with RR tracks, loaded with freight cars. They were only 1½ ft. from the deck to the water line. We tried to sneak onto the scow, but it was watched too closely, so we went to the ferry and bought tickets to a place situated about ten miles from the town of Nelson. We boarded the ferry as soon as we had bought the tickets; we walked around inspecting it. It was a typical river steamboat, with a big paddle wheel in the back. The boat did not sail until 5 p.m., and we had boarded it at noon.

We arrived at Nelson at 9 p.m. We heard that the police in Nelson were very strict, so we bought tickets to Slocan, three stations from Nelson. Crawford had instructed me in the procedure, so when the train stopped at South Slocan, we got off, and wandered slowly along the train towards the engine. I noticed how the train personnel kept watching us, but we paid no attention to them. When we reached the engine, we jumped quickly between the tender and the first boxcar, but alas, the train crew had spotted us, and soon a man came with a lantern in his hand, warning us to get off quickly or take the consequences. Well, there wasn't much we could do about it, so we jumped off again, and soon the train left without us. Unluckily, there was another bum riding the engine tender, and he was chased off too. Boy, was he mad! He bawled the h— out of us. Luckily, a train came along ten minutes later heading for Nelson, so we jumped it and rode back to Nelson. It had cost $1.20, and we were still in Nelson. That night we slept in a hotel, costing me more money. The next day we went down to the station and found out that there would be no train leaving until after dinner.

That afternoon we jumped a freight for Castlegar. The next day we reached Grand Forks, riding on the ladders between two boxcars. It was a cold trip in rainy weather. That night we took a hotel in Grand Forks. The next day we found out that no trains would leave until the next day, so we started walking. We walked twenty-three miles in snow over our ankles. That evening we reached Greenwood. At Greenwood we bought tickets to Midway, from where we, the day after, jumped a freight going to Penticton. We rode in an open freight car, and the whole day we had nothing to eat but coal dust from the engine. We arrived at Penticton that evening. Took another hotel room.

The next morning we went down to the station where we struck up a conversation with an Extra-Gang foreman. He told us that they were going to Princeton that same day. He took pity on us, and that is how it happened that the same afternoon we rode in comfort for sixty miles in a train caboose, sitting beside a warm stove. Before we left, they gave us a hearty supper. At Princeton we caught a freight after waiting only two hours; it took us to Brookmere. Here we had to wait a whole day, and finally the next evening we jumped on the tender of a passenger engine. It went pretty good for awhile, but after a few miles the train was stopped by a snow slide in the mountains. So there we stood in the mountains, shivering from the cold. We stood underneath the engine for a while, but all of a sudden they let loose a great blast of steam right in our faces. When we could stand it no longer, we boarded the train. And when the train finally started moving, we were not discovered by the conductor until we were close to Hope. So I bought tickets to Vancouver, as we were dead tired. We had spent close to $100 since we left Cranbrook, whereas the tickets would have cost us only $56. We took a room in the London hotel, and next day we located a housekeeping room. We have now been looking for work for a month, and found none!

December 20, 1923. Somebody phoned Crawford, saying that some lady wished to speak to him. He went outside to see who it was

and found a couple of young ladies who used to live in a room next to ours. He talked to them a bit, and in the end they asked him to go home to get me. So he came home and got me. We went to the movies. Afterwards I walked one of them home. She said that it probably would be the last time we saw each other. I said that was all right, mostly because I did not know what to say. I do not believe myself that it will be the last time we see each other. Her name is Miss Hamand—nineteen years old.
December 29, 1923. I wrote a letter to Clara Roed. She had written me and wanted to know how I was. At the same time, I asked to get a picture of her. I am assuming she is getting married now.

1924

In 1924, Vancouver and Calgary were still suffering from the post-war depression. The coal fields of Alberta were plagued by chronic under-employment, and crops in the south were devastated by intense drought.

[*Diary*:] January 12, 1924. What a life we lead! We went through all of the month of December and way into January looking for a job, but nothing. I have been to all the big businesses, but no work there at all. Yesterday we went around to the White Lunch restaurants here and were also turned down there, but we just continued. We have enough money to live on until February 4; after that, I do not know.
Vancouver, January 17, 1924. God help me! What will the end be? Still none of us have found a job. Every day now, I have gone up to the White Lunch, and there is nothing to do. We have now $7 left to live on for three people (still my money). We have the room here until February 3. There are not the least prospects for a job. Crawford has samples of shirts costing $6 - 8 apiece, and I know darned well that he will not be able to sell any. Bjarne has a very bad cold, and I'm about out of good humour.

"Lift your head, you healthy lad
What if a hope or two are broken
A new one will gleam in your eye
as soon as it will shine from above."

I hope that is not a lie. A couple of days ago, I had a letter from Maren Johanne, and I answered her right away.

January 18, 1924. It's wonderful how everything can change overnight! Today I was hired by the White Lunch on Pender Street. I start working tomorrow.

A White Lunch restaurant, possibly on Pender St. A neon sign hangs over the front, which is decorated with mosaic tiles and stained glass. Inside, surrounded by white tiled walls, folded cloth napkins in glasses stand on each white tabletop. A steak and potato breakfast is advertised for 20 cents. Vancouver, 1923.
Courtesy VPL, Special Collections, VPL 21458. Photo digitally restored.

January 19, 1924. Today at 10 o'clock a.m., I was at White Lunch and learned that I could come again the day after tomorrow, Monday, at 11 a.m. and start working. If the manager changes his mind, he will phone. Crawford and Bjarne went out to a Danish steamer today. I had heard about it through the Danish consul, and Bjarne has just about got a job there. The steamer is named "Atlanterhavet" [*The Atlantic*] and travels to China. Bjarne is to report Monday at 8 a.m. Crawford still has no job.

January 21, 1924. I was supposed to start working today, but when I got there, I was told they could not use me yet. But I was told to come around at 5 p.m., which I did, and this time I was definitely hired. I'm to start at 10 a.m. tomorrow; the manager will tell me what shift I'll get on. My work will be to clear the tables after the customers have left, wash floors, etc. Bjarne and Crawford are still out of work, but Bjarne has a chance to get on a Danish steamer that is sailing to China. The boat is at anchor out in the harbour, and he'll have to hire a boat and row out to see the captain. Crawford thinks he has a chance to get on a tugboat, working out of Vancouver harbour. I went with another Dane to visit John [*Larsen*] who still has his leg in a cast.

January 22, 1924. Crawford & Bjarne today rowed out to see the captain of the steamer I had heard about from the Danish consulate here in Vancouver. It looks like Bjarne has a good chance to get a job. Crawford is still unemployed.

January 23, 1924. Crawford & Bjarne went out to the boat today, and as Bjarne is still not back, he must have got on. Len was here today. He, Crawford and I sat talking when the phone rang out in the hall. The White Lunch manager wanted me to come down for an hour of practice this afternoon, which I did. It wasn't so hard, and I don't think it will take me very long to learn the routine. I'll get $10 a week with board. I have bought Bjarne's wicker trunk for $1.

January 27, 1924. I have been working in the White Lunch since Monday. I work from 11 or 12 a.m. till 11 p.m. or midnight, with time off from 2:30 to 5 p.m. It is very hard work, especially on the feet, but it's better than no work! Bjarne is working on *The Atlantic*, and is quite satisfied; the boat sails next week. Yesterday was my day off, so I went out to the hospital to visit John. He is O.K., but bored stiff. Crawford is still unemployed.

February 9, 1924. I'm still working at the White Lunch. I'm getting more acquaintances such as a Dane and a Norwegian, but I'm not too happy with them: the Dane is much too Danish and the Norwegian appears to be a liar. Still, I loaned him my last $2. He claims he will soon get a job and pay me back. Somehow I doubt it! As I was working today, I heard someone say, "Hello" behind me. It was Bruce, whom I threshed with. He teaches Piano here in Vancouver. He would like me to move in with him and teach Violin. I don't think it will work. I went up to visit him at his studio this afternoon.

He lives, like other artists, with a woman. Crawford has now got a job on a tugboat, and is therefore away from home. I'm all mixed up these days. John is in the hospital; he has a sweetheart in Denmark who has a child of his, and another sweetheart over here. Crawford, who is living part time with a married woman; the Norwegian, I distrust very much—and Bruce suggests that I move

in with him and start a violin school, but living that kind of wild life does not agree with my principles. Lately, I have had a yearning to go back to the clean prairies, and I have a hunch that's what I'll do.
Vancouver, April 2, 1924. Once I started to work in the White Lunch, I did not find time to keep up my diary. Still, quite a lot has happened. Crawford got a job on a tugboat at $75 a month. He worked for about two months, but he quit a week ago. He says the work was too hard and too long. He's out of work with $4 in his pocket. But that doesn't bother him. He suggested today that he and I go out and dig for gold this spring; we will need to get $80 saved before July. Guess who would do the saving? John is released from the hospital, he gets $65 a month from the Compensation Board, he will be O.K. in another month. Personally, I'm getting along O.K. I had a row with Bob [*his boss?*] today. I'll get a dollar raise per week and get to work behind the counter.
Vancouver, May 8, 1924. I'm still working at the White Lunch. Crawford got himself another job on a boat, getting $90 and board. But we are still working on a plan to take a bunch of tourists up to the Caribou country; we will leave Vancouver on July 10. But no one knows what the future has in store. I haven't heard from my family for over half a year. John is still living with me. It is tough to find pocket money, but he hopes to find work pretty soon.

Vancouver, April 14 to May 30, 1924
Dear Alfred!

It is now five months since I last received a letter from Denmark, although I have written to all of you. Have you all died, or what is wrong? Maybe my letters never reached you? Just to be sure, I will suppose that they didn't get there and start with my arrival at Vancouver in December last year, full of hopes and confidence. My American friend and I took a housekeeping room where we made our own meals while we were constantly looking for work. But there was none to be found, and our small grubstake kept dwindling. Two months went by, and I found myself broke. I had gone for twenty-four hours without eating when I finally landed a job in a restaurant called White Lunch. The first thing they gave me was a great big meal. I then was ordered to get myself a good haircut, and present myself for work next morning. I got $10 a week and my board. I am still working there, but feel that it is about time that I get away and find other work with higher pay.

The White Lunch is a help yourself business where the customers pick out their food from prepared dishes, put it on a tray and sit down at a table to eat it. So there are no waiters, but the staff carry out the dishes, and that was my job for the first month. I have since been promoted to fill cream pitchers, issue butter slabs and make coffee and tea. It is actually a very nice job. We average about 700 - 800 customers every twenty-four hours. We are open day & night.

April 15. I now get $12 a week, and the manager has promised me a counter job as soon as one gets open. If nothing else, it must be a sure sign that my English language is getting better. I speak and think in English when I am with Canadians. It makes me proud when I can tell people that I have been in Canada only a year. Of course, I'm far from perfect. Some take me to be a Scotchman, others a Frenchman, but there is no doubt that the English I learned in Denmark has helped me lot. If you write to Mr. Busk, don't forget to thank him for what he ground into my head at school. What I am most thankful for is that his grammar teaching was so thorough. What I have learned of English grammar has given me an advantage over the ones who have been here the same amount of time. And do tell that to the students at the school. Nobody knows where they will end up in the world, and it is the grammar they learn last in a foreign country.

At present I barely make a living, as I am helping some friends with money and food; they have not been able to find work. But I'll make out all right. If I was to tell you of all the terrible things I have seen here this winter, I could fill a book. And I thank my God for keeping me from falling by the wayside with a lot of other young boys here in Vancouver. There are 200,000 people living here, and of that number there are at least 30,000 unemployed. Those numbers were for March, but it is not very different for April. Many of them are cold and hungry.

I don't know what the future holds for me. Lately, I have been toying with the idea of learning Spanish. I doubt if I'll stay in Canada. Maybe I'll go to South America. I think there are better opportunities there. USA is "no good," "absolutely no good," and I am still travel-itchy. With spring here I can get a job on a farm, in a lumber camp or a restaurant, without starting from the bottom. However, at the present I'm playing around with an idea that my American friend, Crawford, has been pressing me with; he thinks we should advertise ourselves as tourist guides for people are interested in the interior of BC. He has lived up there himself for five years and knows the country very well. He thinks we could made a lot of money on this & would be leaving his job at $95 a month. We must take off from here on July 15. But how the whole thing will come out, only time will tell, but I won't go with him if I'm not sure that it's O.K.

May 29. Please excuse the little break; my arm was tired from writing. I'm still fine, and I work in the same restaurant, because I'm afraid to quit as it's almost impossible to get a job here in town. It's all the immigrants who spoil everything. I'm living with another Dane. He got his leg broken between Christmas & New Year's on board a freight steamer.

Friday, May 30. Excuse another little break, but my hand was hurting again. The other Dane's leg is now recovering, and he's already been looking for work for three weeks, but "nothing doing." I'm helping him as well as I can, and we are getting along. I don't know what I'll do for money this season, but I can't help but go off with Crawford, because that will be just the life I'm longing to try. It will be out in God's free nature, forests, mountains and lakes, with hunting, fishing and camping. And if I find that there's no money in it, I can always go out to the prairie & work at threshing.

Generally, Vancouver is an excellent city with a nice climate. It was not cold all winter, but how it rained! The summer is not too hot, & it only rains once a week. The town is surrounded by big snow covered mountains & the Pacific Ocean. There is a nice beach. Almost every day I go walking out in a big park in the outskirts of the city—Stanley Park. Here you see the big trees for which BC is famous. There are trees which, when hollowed out below, a car could drive through. And then there are all kinds of flora. Oh boy! I'm sure that the botanical garden [*in Denmark*] is nothing compared with that. They sure would be a sight for Alfred's eyes. Among other things, there is a slope about 500 meters long with big stones all over, and among the stones, there are flowers. Some are sort of like carnations, with more varieties than I ever could have dreamed about, and many flowers I don't know at all, from Denmark—[*varieties of*] climbing roses, etc. Among the flowers, I saw one day (I couldn't believe my own eyes) a humming bird. I don't see many butterflies, but may see more when I get up in the mountains.

The town itself is a typical Canadian city with long straight streets and sharp corners. Quite a lot of skyscrapers, but not so

"A picture of me in front of a 'little' tree in Stanley Park."
—Ole Nissen, Vancouver, 1924.

high. The highest is only thirty-two floors. The people are mostly happy and pleasant. The religion is mostly Protestant, but there are lots of Catholics. One branch of the Protestants breaks off to Christian Science. They don't believe in doctors, but say that God will heal them through prayers. Yes, they go so far as to insist that one can recover from a broken leg by putting it together, and then God will heal it through prayers. My hostess belongs to the Christian Scientists, and she does her utmost to convert me. But I keep strongly to the religion of my childhood—with its limits. I'm sorry to confess that I've neglected my church very much, but I think that I'll now have to renew the interest.

My violin playing, strangely enough, often brings me compliments, and I have had more chances to try my luck. The last offer was a three month trip to Alaska, $25 a week & free transportation. But I don't dare to try the artist's luck. I'm staying amateur. Someone offered to buy my violin for $30, but what would I do then? I could sell my stamp album for $20, but what would I tell Mrs. Lange [*an acquaintance in Denmark*]?

Well! I'll now close with my love to you all, and you must excuse my poor tired arm. Now write to 720 Homer St., Vancouver BC! And don't wait as long as I did, please!

Yours sincerely, Helge

Write H. Chris Nissen. Canadians can't pronounce Helge, so I'm calling myself Chris.

[*Diary*:] Sunday, June 1, 1924. I worked at White Lunch until 5 p.m. At that time, Len and John came to pick me up. We then went over to North Vancouver. A wonderful trip. It took twenty minutes by ferry. From North Vancouver, we went by streetcar to Capilano Canyon. Here we first went to the Suspension Bridge, a long bridge which hangs on four steel wires. When you walk on it, it rocks like a boat in water. It is about 300 metres long and 1½ metres wide. Underneath, deep down, you see rocks and a foaming stream which makes a lot of noise. Afterwards we went to another part of Capilano Canyon. First we went to a viewing platform, which was way up on a cliff side, and way down the stream was roaring against the rocks. After that we went down to the river and came right down to a big waterfall. Oh, how beautiful!
June 3, 1924. Still working at White Lunch. Crawford still working on the same boat. John has for more than three weeks looked for work from 7 every morning, but nothing doing. I have started having strong doubts about the success of Crawford's plans and am contemplating quitting my job here and going back to the prairies with John. But I have still not talked to Crawford and dread meeting him. Maybe he has already spent $15 on advertising. But John is trying to cheat compensation out of $30 more, and if he gets it, we are leaving, whatever.
Vancouver, Monday, June 9, 1924. Today I quit my job at the White Lunch, and John & I are leaving for the prairie. Right now I have $43 in my pocket, and John hasn't a cent. The fare to Calgary is $26.50 for each of us, so there is no choice but to try to ride the freight again. I'm sure not looking forward to it.
Westminster, BC, June 13, 1924. John & I started our journey east today. We bought a ticket to here, and we plan on catching a freight from here. Prospects are not very good; they claim they have a very cranky cop here. We got on the way by 11:30 p.m. We jumped on a flat car in between two lumber cars. We were fairly well sheltered. The train stopped every hour to take on water and coal. The train crew walked up and down the train, but every time they came near, we hid in some holes in the timber. At Mission, the first major stop, the train stopped for an hour. They changed engines, and away we went again. We travelled all night, and next morning at 9 a.m. we arrived at Pinatan. Here they stopped for an hour,

and then went on until we reached North Bend, where we jumped off.

North Bend and onward, June 14, 1924. At this time, we had had nothing to eat since yesterday at 4 p.m., so we were good and hungry. We therefore walked up town and tried to find a place to eat. North Bend is entirely populated with CPR personnel, but, of course, we did not know that. We finally found what we thought might be a restaurant, but the place was closed.

We went around looking for the Chinaman to [*open the café*] for supper. All of a sudden, we were confronted by a CPR policeman who asked us if we were on the freight that had just arrived. We had to admit it, because our faces and clothes showed all the smoke and coal dust we had collected. He asked us if we had any revolvers on our persons. Then he said, "Well, I like boys that tell the truth, and you two had better hurry out of this place, but don't jump the freight inside the yard, or you'll get caught sure as h- - -!" He also suggested that we get something to eat, as our train would be stopped for an hour or so. We thanked him very much and continued on our search for the Chinaman. Finally, we found him, but boy! What a sight—his face was covered with blood, and it was easy to see that he had been in a fight. We asked him if he could give us something to eat, but he did not answer us, and disappeared again.

We then started for the RR tracks again; on the way, we met a couple other bums, but we did not stop to talk to them. We walked on past the yard limit where we lay down and waited for a train to come. But after ten minutes or so, a man came along. He asked us what was the idea of half-killing the Chinaman. We got pretty scared, and told him that we had nothing to do with it. However, he ordered us to come with him to face the Chinaman. On the way, we met the CPR police, who said the "mountain police" wanted to keep us as suspects. But after a long conference, they let us go. Boy, were we happy. We went back to wait for a train. Ten minutes later, a train came along, and we weren't slow in jumping it. We rode on the ladders in between two boxcars. What an awful ride in the mountains, crawling up steep hills, through long tunnels, downhill at a fast clip, around sharp curves. We had to hang on for our lives, but we finally arrived at Kamloops that afternoon at 4 o'clock. We had been without food for over twenty-four hours, so we had a big meal at Kamloops. After the meal, we lay down by the Fraser River and had a good sleep until 8 p.m.

when we walked up town where we had coffee and some bread. Then we walked back to the station. Originally, we had been sorry to leave our train, for the sake of getting something to eat. So imagine our happy surprise to find our old train just ready to pull out. We found a dark spot to cross the tracks, and when we got to the train, we found a couple of tank cars that appeared quite suitable. Five minutes later, the train pulled out.

Kamloops to Revelstoke, June 15, 1924. We rode the whole night and reached Revelstoke next morning at 10 a.m. We could see it was a big point, so we jumped off before the train reached the Yards. We walked up town and got something to eat. Then we walked around the town to the outskirts and lay down, waiting for the next train. The first two trains were passenger trains—they were going too fast to jump. Finally, at 3 p.m. a freight came along, and we jumped on a tank car that took us all the way to Glacier where we arrived at 6 p.m. The train did not go any farther, and again we found ourselves in a little CPR town. But there were no police here, and the train crew paid no attention to us. We found a store and bought some doughnuts and argued about where we should stay until the next train came along. The result was that we got mad, and each went his own way. It took us two hours to find

The route through which Ole rode the freights in 1923 and 1924. CPR train at Field, BC, near Connaught Tunnel, 1925. —Courtesy, BCA, D-08469.

each other again. We laid down in an old abandoned box car, where we slept until 11:30 p.m. (2½ hours). John heard a train coming, and we reached it just in time to jump into a lumber car.
Glacier to Field, June 16, 1924. We now travelled through the [*Connaught*] Tunnel, (½ hour, fifteen miles long). Before long we fell asleep and did not wake up until it was daylight. What really woke us was the fact that the train had stopped. My watch had also stopped, and we had no idea what time it was. We waited in the boxcar for around three hours, when I felt that I'd had enough, and we jumped down from the boxcar to investigate. We met a section man who told us that it was 1 p.m. and that we were in the town of Field, BC, which, being a division point, was full of railway cops. We therefore chose a walk around the perimeter of the town and got to the other end of the railway station, where we waited for another freight train. None showed up until 8 p.m., when we luckily found another empty boxcar, and travelled the whole night.
Field to Calgary, June 17, 1924. Next morning we arrived in Calgary at 7 a.m., without any further trouble. We then walked uptown, where we got something to eat and found a room where we slept until 5 p.m. We then took in a show and went early to bed. The whole trip had cost us 80¢, and we still have $75 in our pockets.
Calgary, June 20, 1924. We have now walked around Calgary looking for work for three days, without any luck. But today John landed a job at Trochu, and I decided to go to Hussar after I had phoned Clifgard, the storekeeper there. He thought he could find me something if I could get there.
Calgary to Hussar, June 21, 1924. Took the train to Bassano at 1:55 a.m. and arrived there at 4 a.m. There did not appear to be any work there, so I went on to Hussar where I arrived at 12:35 p.m. when I went to see Mr. Clifgard. Ten minutes after my talk with him, he asked one of his customers if he had got the hired man he was looking for. The man said, "no," and Clifgard introduced me to Frank Kelly, who offered me $50 a month to drive seven horses, pulling a plow.[11] His farm is eleven miles north of town, and on my arrival there he introduced me to his youngsters; the oldest boy is seventeen, and will also work in the field with me.

---

11 Frank Kelly was formerly a noted hard-rock mine engineer who worked throughout the Americas and lost everything in the 1906 San Francisco earthquake. Because of a lung disease, he and his family turned to agriculture, first in Washington in 1910; then, in 1917, they moved to the Wintering Hills where they farmed successfully.

Frank Kelly and children, Hussar, 1924.

Sun., June 22, 1924. I'm now settled down at Kelly's, and today I borrowed a saddle horse and rode over to visit Bob Halsey who lives three miles east of here. But Bob wasn't home, so I went back to Kelly's.

Mon., June 23, 1924. Started to plow with seven horses; one of them was a colt that had never been in harness before. We got along pretty well.

Tues., June 24, to Sat., June 28, 1924. Spent the week plowing and fixing fences.

Sun., June 29, 1924. We branded three colts during the forenoon. In the afternoon, Francis and I rode over to Jack Morton's and watched their Stampede, quite a thrill! [12]

Mon., June 30, to Sat., July 5, 1924. Plowed all week.

---

12 Jack Morton was legendary in southern Alberta. In 1896 he was sent by his parents in Manitoba to help with the herds of cattle on their great ranch near Rosebud and the Red Deer River. A big man, Morton, at age twenty, weighed about 250 pounds and stood six foot three. In 1900 he moved to Gleichen, west of Hussar. Later, he began his own ranch, the CX, and, in 1919, the famous Two Bar. Stories about Morton abound, such as his sending a bear cub to his family at the Two Bar, lassoing a "Red Light" tent near the Calgary stampede, surprising the occupants, and humming a little tune while receiving surgery after a knife wound. In 1923 the crops were wonderful, but grain prices fell. It is said that Morton threshed 93,000 bushels of wheat on his Indian Springs farm and lost it all to the banks.

Sun., July 6, 1924. Received my suitcase from Vancouver.
Mon., July 7, to Sat., July 12, 1924. Plowed all week.
Sun., July 13, 1924. Just "laid around" all day.
Mon., July 14, to Sat., July 19, 1924. Plowed all week.
Sun, July 20, 1924. Today I borrowed a saddle horse and rode over to Larsen's, where Axel is still working. Larsen went to Hussar, and Axel and I talked all day.
Mon., July 21, 1924. Drove Francis & Lois, some of the Kelly kids, over to the Lawson Range, where we picked berries, (Saskatoons and blackberries). We had picked for an hour when it started to rain, and it kept raining, so we had to drive back home again. When we got to the farm, Mr. Kelly told me that my month was up and he would drive me back to Hussar and pay my wages. His crop was dried up so bad that he could not afford to keep a hired hand. In the evening, I helped him castrate pigs.
Tues., July 22, 1924. Mr. Kelly drove me to Hussar, where he paid me the $50, and gave me a good recommendation. I went to Clifgard, and asked him to help me again about a job. He said he would do the best he could.
Wed., July 23,1924. No news; stayed at the Chinaman's.[13] Bored-stiff!
Thurs., July 24, 1924. Still no news. Staying with the Chinaman. Farmers suffering from the drought, no money for Labourers!
Fri., July 25, 1924. Still no job. Took in a show and a dance tonight, got to bed at 4 a.m.
Sat., July 26, 1924. Still no job! Getting very discouraged, it is too expensive to stay at the Chinaman's.
Sun., July 27, 1924. I went to visit Larsen's. Had a good time. In the afternoon Clifgard came out, and told me that he had found me a job. It is for Harper's Ranch. I'll stay at Larsen's tonight and go back to Hussar in the morning; the Ranch foreman will come and get me.
Mon., July 28, 1924. Returned to Hussar; no one came for me!
Tues., July 29, 1924. Still no one came for me. I played Black-Jack all afternoon.
Wed., July 30, 1924. Walked around Hussar looking for a man who

[13] John Chang moved to Hussar about 1920. In his cafe, Chang greeted customers with, "Apple pie, raisin pie—apple pie all gone—what'll you have?" Around his marble-topped tables, local people got together for coffee and news. Chang curled and made generous donations to the community, moving away in 1932 when his establishment burned down.

was going towards the North. Saw "Shorty" Westover.[14] Found a man who lives four miles from Harper's ranch and got a ride with him, walked the rest of the way.[15] Arrived at Harper's 5 p.m. and asked for the foreman [*Walter Schang*]. When I found him, I told him that Clifgard had told me I might find a job here. He hired me. I went around and got acquainted with the other men (9). Had supper and was shown where to sleep.

Sun., August 11, 1924. Still working at Harper's. It is a large ranch, 3,230 acres with wheat. It has been raining the last week. It will

Friends at Harper's ranch—man, far left, unknown; Walter Schang, foreman; the next three, probably, are: Mrs. Harper, Amy Thew, and Ed Harper. Woman, far right, and child, unknown. Early 1920s. —Courtesy, Gary Schang.

---

[14] G. (Bert) Westover moved to Alberta from Portage La Prairie, Manitoba, in 1903 at age fifteen, to work at various jobs. After serving overseas in WW 1, and being awarded two medals, he returned. In 1922 he and his wife rented a farm northeast of Hussar. They moved again in 1931.

[15] Ed Harper and his wife emigrated from the States, settling on two sections of land north of Hussar by the spring of 1918. Walter Schang, foreman, was an intelligent, thoughtful man and would be an important part of father's life for the next six years. Walter had been foreman at a Seattle shipyard, where, during a strike, he was approached by Dart Sewell, a CPR land agent. From this contact, Walter and his brother, Harold, from Indiana, both bachelors, moved to Hussar in 1919, jointly buying two sections north of Harper's ranch. There the Schangs farmed, broke land for Harper and other settlers, and built their own small house.

take a couple of weeks before we can start harvesting. Last week one of the men was fired as there isn't much to do until harvest time. The last week I have helped the blacksmith, helped to chop oats, shoveled 1,000 bushels of oats, etc. It is too wet to work in the field. The ranch has seventy work horses, fifteen saddle horses, three engines [*tractors*], one separator, seven binders, twelve wagons and nine hired men. We have very fine meals. It's good here.

<u>Sat., September 20, 1924</u>. I'm still working for Harper. I've driven a binder the last three weeks at $3.50 a day. We have started threshing now ($4 a day). I'm driving a real good team of horses, but the weather has been bad the last two weeks. We worked only three full days.

<u>Sat., September 27, 1924</u>. Good threshing weather; working "full speed."

<u>Mon., October 8, 1924</u>. We have been idle for a week on account of rain. We hope we may start up again tomorrow. Two of the wheat-haulers have quit. Harper demanded that they should haul grain in rainy weather. I think I'll stay on the job as chores-boy during the winter.

The other day I went to Bassano and had a tooth pulled.

<u>Sat., October 23, 1924</u>. Finished threshing; had earned $220 since I started working for Harper. I had drawn $50, and was paid the balance; I took off for Calgary travelling with young Norwegians.

<u>Calgary, October 25 to 28, 1924</u>. Have been bumming around Calgary; no jobs, took in some shows; bought a watch and some clothes. Spent $70; took off for Edmonton late at night.

<u>Fri., October 29, 1924</u>. Arrived at Edmonton 8.30 a.m. On the way, I met an old friend from my White Lunch days in Vancouver. Told him how things stood with me. He told me about the mines at Sterco [*south of Edson*]; there are three camps of coal mining, and he thought sure that there would be work there. I suggested it to my companions [*the Norwegians*], but they wanted none of it. Still, I decided to try it. The train left Edmonton at 1 p.m. and the ticket cost me $7. Arrived at Edson 6 p.m. Took in a show in the evening.

<u>Sat., October 30, 1924</u>. Took off for Sterco; arrived by 2 p.m. Went up to the bunkhouses. At supper time, I went with the men to the dining house; the meal cost me 50¢. I asked the cook if he could get me a flunky-job—no! so I went back to the bunkhouses. The men there told me that my chances of getting a job were very slim. The Company was working with only a ¼ crew.

Sterco, November 2, 1924. Have now been here four days, and have been all over, looking for work, but "nothing doing." There are three camps here, four miles apart. The camp where I'm staying is a surface mine where they use large steam shovels to dig out the coal. The third camp is an underground mine where they employ Union labour. It costs $50 to join the Union, and I was informed that there was absolutely no opening for the next two - three weeks. Tomorrow the train goes back to Edmonton, and I'll try and get some work in a tie camp somewhere. I still have $70 left, but it doesn't look very encouraging. There is seven inches of snow, and it is 10 below F.

November 3, 1924. Left Sterco today and heading for Junkins [*later named Wildwood*], where I'll try to get some work in the tie camps; will have to stay here in Edson tonight.

8 p.m. Soon discovered some new complications are waiting for me! First, there is no train leaving for Junkins tomorrow; I'll have to wait until Weds. 10 a.m. Well, I then tried to phone Swanson, the owner of a tie camp, but he wasn't home. I've just found out that there is a tie camp here, close to Edson. Will try and find more out about it tomorrow. In the afternoon, saw a show, "First out from Broadway."

Edson, Tues., November 4, 1924. Today I tried to locate the owner of the camp at Edson, but found out that he lives thirty miles out of town and that's too far for me to walk, so I'll forget about it. They say that it is hard to get a job in Junkins, but I'm going to try anyway. Have $58 left. Did not do too much today; wrote a letter to Alfred, but I won't send until I have a job.

Junkins, Wed., November 5, 1924. Hurray! It looks like Mother Fortune has not completely forgotten me. I think our chances here are quite good. Left Edson at noon. Arriving here, I went into the grocery store and talked to a Swede. He told me there was a tie camp eighteen miles out, and he was sure I could get a job there. I stayed in a Swedish hotel that night.

Thurs., November 6, 1924. Today I walked with two other men out to the Swanson-Corser Company. It was twenty-two miles. Arrived there at 5 p.m. Shortly after met the foreman, Corser, and asked him about the chances for a job. He looked quite anxious. Finally, he asked me if I could cut logs. I told him that I had never tried it before but was sure it would not take me long to learn. Then he took me into his office and sold me an axe, a file, a yardstick, etc., handed me a saw. He will pay 6 cents a log, 8 feet long and at least

8 ½ inches thick. I also bought two blankets ($15), have $25 left. Will sleep here tonight; will walk to camp tomorrow (five miles).

Edson, November 5, 1924
Dear Gudrun & Alfred:

I still haven't heard a word from Denmark. I wonder why? If I did not know Alfred, Johannes and Maren J. better, I would think that somehow you had forgotten I existed. If that was so, I would get very angry and break all connections. But I know for sure that you would have answered my letters under any circumstances. However, I know for a fact that I have heard from *nobody* since last New Year. I know that I have sent at least four letters home. Of course, I haven't stayed in one place more than three months, so that may have had something to do with it, but I always left a forwarding address. However, I owe you who have done so much for me a report of what I have been doing even if I have no idea how things are with you.

If I remember correctly, I wrote my last letter, while I was working for the farmer, Mr. Kelly, at Hussar. I worked there for only a month because he could not afford me on account of the drought; the harvest was very poor. However, a week later I got a job on a large ranch, where I earned $50 a month until harvest (three weeks). During the harvest, I drove a binder ($3.50) for twenty-one days, after which I worked on a threshing rig, where I earned $4 a day for twenty-seven days. We finished up on my birthday October 21. I then took off for Calgary with $160 in my pocket.

I stayed in Calgary for three days without looking for work. All I could think of was REST after twenty-seven days of darned *hard* work from 4:30 in the morning to 7:30 in the evening. But after the three days, I started to look for work, but it was harder to find than I had anticipated. I then took off for Edmonton (250 miles north), after spending $65 in one week in Calgary. On arrival in Edmonton, I went to the Unemployment Office there, where I received the same results as in Calgary.

However, I stayed in Edmonton only one day, as I met an old friend from Vancouver, who told me about fair opportunities in the Sterco Coal Mines 160 miles west of here. So we took off for Sterco, where we found to our disgust that the machinery had broken down and half of the men had to be laid off. So again I had to look elsewhere. I then went to Edson, where I'm writing this letter. The lumber camps here have more men than they need. I will go to Junkins tomorrow where there is a Swedish lumber camp. At present I still have $70 in my pocket. This is an outline of what I've been doing since last New Year. Now as to my health: I have not had a sick day since I left Denmark. This harvest, however, I got my nose badly busted. This is how it happened.

During the threshing, I was pitching bundles on my bundle wagon. We had ten wagons, and nearly all the horses were mares with colts. My team was a gelding and a mare with colt. The colt was a real pet; I had him trained to lift his front foot when I asked him. If he got in my road, I would tap with my fork, and he would get out of my road; but one day a colt from another wagon came over to visit him, and I didn't realize it; so when a colt stood in my road, I gave him the usual tap with my bundle fork, with an instant reply. Before I knew what had happened, I was laying on the ground with the blood pouring from my nose. The colt had kicked the fork, and the handle hit across my nose and eye. A thing like that would never have happened if I had realized it was a different colt instead of the one I was used to. I left my team and wagon, with my hand over my nose. I did not realize that the blood was running just as fast as if I had put my hand in the pocket. The cook bandaged my nose and eye; she said that the hole was at least a half inch deep in my nose. Anyway, I went back to work and finished the day. It is now five weeks since it happened, and I still have a bad scar.

During harvest I developed a bad toothache, until I finally had to go to the nearest dentist a distance of thirty miles and back on a saddle horse to get the tooth pulled out. And when harvest was finished, I went to the dentist again and got my whole mouth overhauled: it cost me $50. I'm telling now, only to explain the reasons I spent so much money in Calgary. I had nine teeth filled and all the teeth cleaned and polished. They really look handsome now! And if it hadn't been for the nose, I would look fairly presentable now.

However, to get back to realities. I have now been here in Canada nineteen months and I haven't even got *started* to make that fortune I had dreamed of when I left Denmark. I'm beginning to realize that I will never amount to much this way. However, I haven't got much money, so it is not so easy to make new plans. A friend of mine suggested that I look into the creamery trade. He said that he could get me started next spring at $50 a month plus board. It would be nice to get into something steady!

I'm writing this letter from Edson, and I won't mail it until I get myself a job for the winter, *so you will be able to write me a letter back.*

Junkins, Alta., November 16. I must get this letter on the way! As I told you, I went from Edson to Junkins. The next day, I walked out to the camp by myself. It took me the whole day. I found the foreman and asked him for a job. He asked me if I had had any experience. Oh sure! So he gave me a saw; I had to buy my own axe, file, etc. Then he showed me the place where I was to saw down trees and make them into logs.

I was on that job only two days when I was handed a team of horses, and I am now hauling logs from the cutting place to the saw mill. It is very hard work. We work from 7 a.m. to 6 p.m.; it is completely dark both morning and night. We get up at 5 o'clock and to bed at 9 p.m. The wages are $3.10 a day less $1.10 for board. I have never worked so hard in all my life, but it is better to hang onto the job. There is not very much chance of getting another. So I'll stay here this winter and hope to receive a letter from you (X-mas letter). I send my best and wish you health and happiness.

Helge

Address: H. Chris Nissen, Camp 2
c/o Frank Corser, Junkins, Alta.

[*Diary*:] Fri., November 7, 1924. Walked from Camp 1 after breakfast; came to Camp 2; arrived at 10 a.m. Waited here for the foreman, Crawford. He arrived here at 11:30 a.m.; he gave me a saw, and I was busy sharpening it until 3 p.m. We then walked out to the place where I'm to saw down trees. I worked there till 6 p.m., and walked back to camp. I had made six logs (36¢); it was awful hard work. First you saw the tree down, then you chop the branches off; some of them are awful thick. Next, the tree is sawed in logs, 8 feet long, and you mark your No. on one end (my number is 22), and then you go to the next tree. There is only one bunkhouse for thirty-two men; I sleep in the same bunk with a Finn.[16]

Sat., November 8, 1924. Have been cutting logs all day; dead-tired! Have cut 44 logs today. Getting encouragement from the other men;

---

16 The Corser bunkhouses were built of rough lumber covered on the outside with tarpaper. To generate heat in a hurry, most were equipped with air-tight heaters. The bunks were made of lumber with hay mattresses.—Evelyn Hill, *Where The Lobstick Flows*, (Chip Lake Historical Society, 1987), p. 40.

doing good for a "Greenhorn." The best men can cut 70 to 80 logs a day.

Sun., November 9, 1924. Was idle today; the other log-cutters did not go out either. Read some magazines somebody lent me.

Mon., November 10, 1924. Was just going out to my job, when the foreman for the sawmill came and asked me if I wanted to drive a team skidding logs. The pay was $3.10 a day with board. I thought it over, and took the job. I was given two good horses and a sleigh. I then drove out to the mill and started my job. I drove out in the woods where a helper and I loaded 5 - 8 logs on the sleigh. I then hauled them to the mill and unloaded them on a set of "skids," and went back for another load. It is very hard work to handle those logs, and hard on your clothes.

Thurs., November 20, 1924. Was sick today. Have been working at my new job steady, and will be at it tomorrow again. In the afternoon the foreman came and asked me to work on the mill. I then worked from 3 p.m.

Fri., November 21, 1924. Went back to my hauling job. Today one of the log cutters cut his knee with his axe. He hit the kneecap, and we could see a big open wound. He was a Norwegian. We told him that there was nothing he could do but go to the hospital. But he laughed at us. He asked for some iodine, which he poured over the sore, then he took a needle and proceeded to sew up the wound with common thread. Boy! Did he have strong nerves!

Sat., November 22, 1924. The Norwegian's leg got worse during the night, and we talked him into some sense this morning. He borrowed a horse & sleigh and drove in to Junkins. In my spare time, I have made myself a chessboard, and had some great sessions here.

Sun., November 23, 1924. Wrote letters today and played the violin a man had brought along; it wasn't a very good instrument. Mine is still in Vancouver.

Tues., November 25, 1924. Worked hard today; all three teams had a lot of bad luck today. My sleeping partner went away too, so I'm sleeping alone now.

Fri., December 12, 1924. I'm still working in the tie camp. My work now at the sawmill is to carry slabs.

Thurs., December 25, 1924. Still working at the same place. No Christmas celebration here! Just another day. Work is very hard.

1925

Father worked at the tie camp in Junkins, later called Wildwood, for nine weeks and, by summer, was back on the prairies.

[*Diary*:] Mon., January 16, 1925. I'm still at Junkins, but no longer working on the sawmill. I'm working in Camp 1, with short-haul until February 1.

Junkins, February 16, 1925
Dear Gudrun & Alfred!

I have received your registered letter, for which I heartily thank you! Today is Sunday. Last Wednesday word came from the Post Office for me to authorize sending the letter to the Camp. I did that and the letter arrived Saturday. This letter will be sent tomorrow. This letter [*father's, to Alfred*] should be enough proof for the Bank in Denmark that I am alive; so now I have a small savings account in Denmark that can always come in handy![17]

I have otherwise not much news to tell you since my letter three weeks ago. I am still working for the same outfit, doing same work. I hope I can stay here until April 1. I will go back to the prairie again and work until May 1, at which time I hope to get a job in a creamery.[18]

Love to all from Helge

[*Diary*:] Fri., February 27, 1925. Still working in Junkins, but seriously thinking about leaving. We have to haul the ties such a long distance and are putting in some awful long hours. I have written about some farm work at another place.
Sat., February 28, 1925. Today I have the job as barn boss, though it is only for today. I got up at 4 a.m. and to bed at 9 p.m.
Sun., March 1, 1925. Today I got a new horse instead of Pat who sprained her foot. I have given money to a man who explained that he had to beg until he can get a wooden leg.
Mon., March 2, 1925. Today I had Darky instead of Pat. He went fine with King.
Tues., March 3, 1925. Had Darky again in the morning, but in the afternoon Corser sold a horse, and I had to give Darky to another

---

17 This was from a small inheritance from father's Aunt Larsen in Denmark.

18 Denmark was once an exporter of grain, but due to competition from North America in the 19th century, Danes turned to dairy products—hence father's interest.

man. Got Nigger instead. Nigger is the laziest horse who ever walked on four legs. Had a lot of trouble with him.

Wed., March 4, 1925. Used King and Nigger today again, but I have so much trouble with Nigger that I told Frank [*Corser*] that he would have to either give me another horse or my time. The road through the woods is so badly cut up by the heavy sleds that also use it. Yesterday was one of the warmest days yet. Frank told me that he would try and get me another horse and added that I did not need to haul such big loads, as my horses were much smaller than the others.

Thurs., March 5, 1925. Today I got a different horse, and it was just like a kid getting unexpected candy! I'm hauling ties all alone now. The rest haul from Camp 3, 9 miles from Camp 1, and they have to skid and load their own ties, so I'm lucky I go only 3 ½ miles from camp. Today I was back by 11 a.m. Went back 12:30 and returned 4:30 p.m. In the evening, Corser asked me to exchange horses with Sullivan—I would be getting a slower horse. I said all right, and a half hour later, he asked me to change sleighs with Thomson—I would be getting a narrow sleigh and must haul in wide sleigh tracks. I said that I would try it.

Late in the evening, Starky Beach [*a camp sawyer*] suggested that I come with them to Bruce, Alberta [*southeast of Edmonton*]. They were leaving next Monday. Beach would like to go to Edmonton tomorrow, and have me driving his four horses Sat. & Mon. and then drive one of his outfits to Edmonton (2 ½ days trip). I said all right. He promised me that if he could not get me a job on the prairie, it would not cost me a cent for board and room until I did get a job. And there were three creameries in the neighbourhood. I thought those were pretty good conditions. After I had gone to bed, Jim Ferguson asked me to change horses with him. I told him to take what he wanted as I was quitting tomorrow anyway.

Fri., March 6, 1925. This morning I went part way with Beach to see how his team behaved. They are all fine drivers! After he had passed the bridge, I jumped off and walked back again. I then went in to see Corser and told him that he could exchange my outfit as much as he wanted as I was quitting. He took it quite coolly, and in our conversation we realized that I was the fifth senior worker in the camp, though I had worked only four months. He would have liked to have me stay a little longer, but I'd had enough. Went back to the tent and packed my clothes.

Sat., March 7, 1925. Took Beach's outfit to Corser's Landing [*two miles west of Junkins*]; it went good. I had the largest horses in the camp. Saw a train for the first time in four months.
Sun., March 8, 1925. Didn't do much today. There was a big concert last night; we all sang and played. This morning I curried the four horses; it took me an hour. Beach never bothered to curry his horses. There has been some sickness among the horses in the camp lately. Beach had a horse—(Curly); it died of colic. Thomson had a horse die on him yesterday. He had just hitched it to the sleigh, when it lay down. He got it up again and took it to the barn, and it laid down again. In five minutes, it was dead, colic. There are a lot of South Americans in the camp. There is a lot of talk about the U.S. capitalists building three or four railways in South America. I should look further into it; apparently it isn't so cold in Argentina.
Thursday, March 9, 1925. Have driven Beach's teams for three days. We, Actor and I, left the camp together with seven other men. Altogether, we brought thirty-one horses with us. I had earned $102 since I came to Corser in November.
Bruce, Sun., April 12, 1925. Am now on Beach's farm. Since leaving Junkins, I have worked on his farm for board. I have only $25 left of the $100. But I have bought myself a new suit and boots. Well! We left Junkins in a good mood, but we had a hard trip. It took three days; we arrived in Edmonton Sunday at midnight. We took our horses down to the Penn Coal Mine where Beach has the other outfit working. There was a big, roomy barn. We lay down and slept on the floor. Next morning, Beach arrived, and I gave him my outfit. I stayed in Edmonton that day, and next day Beach and I left Edmonton for Bruce.

Another difficult trip. I only drove two horses on this trip. I had a load of furniture. The others overturned twice, and I overturned twice with the furniture, but nothing was damaged. It rained, snowed and stormed. The worst was that the snow blew so badly that the road was covered. It took 3 ½ days to travel ninety-five miles. When we finally reached Bruce, we were dead tired and sleepy, but here in Bruce this was waiting for us: a dance in honour of Beach's and Myrtle's marriage. So however tired we were, we had to go to the dance, and we danced all night until 5 in the morning. The following week we spent getting acclimatized, and now we are just waiting for the land to be dry enough for plowing. The snow has disappeared, and there is mud all over. On Thursday I am going to Viking to try to get a job in the creamery.

Bruce, Mon., April 13, 1925. Did nothing special except chores. Beach sold a load of bundles for $2 and could therefore afford to go to a dance at Bruce. So at 9 in the evening went to town in our buggy and danced until 4 in the morning. I had fun, but it was a hard trip both there and home. I met Actor at the dance and lent him another $2.50. It will be $5.50 in all. Got home at 5 o'clock.

Bruce, Tues., April 14, 1925. Slept until 12 noon. Got up and did chores. Then Myrtle said that Beach, who had gone to Holden, wanted me to drive Myrtle over to Hammermaster's. They were going to slaughter a pig. But the weather was so stormy that she gave up the trip. Beach came home at 7 o'clock, and the first thing he asked was if we had the pig slaughtered. When he learned that neither one of us had been over there, he got furious and rushed out to the stables, saddled his horse and tore off. This morning he had been to Holden to borrow enough money to carry through the spring, *he says*.

Wed., April 15, 1925. Went to Bruce today. Got four letters from Junkins (three from Denmark). And my violin from Vancouver. It is a bit rusty, but I will get it tuned again.

Thurs., April 16, 1925. Was with Mr. Moore at Viking today. We drove there in Beach's buggy; we arrived at Viking around noon. We had dinner and went uptown doing errands. After that, Moore went and tinkered around with the plow he had come for, and I went to the creamery. I asked for the manager and learned that he had not yet returned from dinner. Then I went up to his home and rang the doorbell. He came out and asked me in. I told him why I had come, and he was very friendly, but he said he was afraid I was too late. He had already got the men he needed. However, he had two new men who would rather sit around smoking a pipe than work. Therefore I gave him my address and Hammermaster's phone number, and he said that maybe he could use me around May 1.

We did not leave Viking until 3 o'clock. Moore drove the plow and I, the buggy. I was at home at 8 o'clock. Beach was at Ryan's and did not get home until 9 o'clock. When he came, we agreed to go to a dance at Bruce, and off we went. We danced until 1:30, and I have never had as much fun at a dance as that time. Went to bed at 3 o'clock.

Fri., April 17, 1925. Got up at 10:30 a.m. Did not do much. It rained all day. Went to bed at 10.

Sat., April 18, 1925. It rained (dripped) onto my bed all last night. Got up at 8 a.m. Went out and chopped some wood. On my way in, I stepped on a board which had a rusty nail sticking up, got the nail more than ½ inch up into my foot. Hurt a lot. Went out to the barn to clean it out. It was 12 o'clock before I had finished all the chores. Came in. Beach and Myrtle were still in bed. Called them. Four and one-half hours without lunch. My foot hurt terribly. Put a hot compress of potatoes and flour on it.

9 p.m. My foot hurt so much I cannot put any weight on it. We washed it in hot water.

Sun., May 10, 1925. It went as I thought: I could not get along with Starky Beach. I plowed for him for eleven days at $45 a month, then we had an argument and I asked for my money. I am now at Mr. Ryan's; and I am sick, a really bad cold. The other day, I was with Mr. Ryan at Holden and asked for work at the creamery there, but chances were not good there either. If I do not soon get a job in a creamery, I will give it up for this year and work in the forest this winter. Right now I have $25.

Hussar, Sun., July 26, 1925. Working for Walter Schang again. Since leaving Starky, I have worked at Irricana for a disabled priest. The work was way too hard, so I came here. I have been working different jobs. The longest time I spent swamping [*dragging*]

Ole operated the plows pulled behind this Caterpillar. Schang outfit, north of Hussar, late 1920s.

seven plows after the Caterpillar. I worked nights from 7 p.m. until 6 a.m.

Sun., Aug. 2, 1925. Hussar. Still working for Walter. I am now doing roadwork at $3 per day. I plow. We are two gangs, and we are always arguing. Was in a fight last Friday, fought a married man, thirty-eight years old. Got a bit of a nosebleed. He called me a thief for stealing his newspaper. He was lying, and when I asked him to retract his words, he walked up to me and hit me and made me furious. He was a boxer, but my youth helped me and took his breath away. I gave him a couple in the head, and he apologized. That is the second fight I have had in Canada. Here they fight almost every evening. Am getting friendly with a New Zealander who just arrived in Canada. He gives me good information on New Zealand. If I have $400 after harvest, I will go there.

Hussar, Alta. Aug. 2, 1925
Dear Gudrun & Alfred:

It is a long time since I last wrote you a letter, and I haven't heard from you either. No matter how hard I tried, I could not get a job in a creamery last spring. I'm now working on the same ranch where I worked last year. I worked for several other farmers before coming back here, but somehow I wasn't satisfied. I like this ranch fine. I work nights from 7 p.m. to 6 a.m. I'm working a seven unit plow, pulled by a large Caterpillar tractor. We are a two man team, the engineer and I. I'm quite happy with my job; there is not the terrible daytime heat and dust, although the mosquitoes are pretty bad, up until midnight. The biggest handicap is the heat while we try to sleep during the day. I always wake up at 12 noon and never seem to get more than 5 - 6 hours sleep, but I have one night free each week, and then I sleep both day and night. We will be finished plowing in a week's time. We will then start getting the binders ready for harvest.

It looks like we will get a real good harvest this year, and good money to be made. Should I make $400 this harvest, I may travel to New Zealand for the winter. The harvest starts down there in December, and you know that New Zealand is a great dairy country. The ticket costs $150; the journey will last three weeks. If I'm unable to go to New Zealand, I will probably go back to the tie camps again this winter. I can't really say that I'm tired of Canada, but I would like to see other lands and look for better opportunities, if any!

My health? Excellent! Humour? O.K. In love? No! Homesick? (pardon me) no! —since I started here in Canada. The violin? Goes good, but is in need of repairs now. I wish I could get in some practice with a piano. Literature? Not much good; I read a few magazines. A few weeks ago, I was in Calgary and spent $40 at the Stampede. It sure was worth seeing! I can't begin to explain all the details to you; it will have to wait until sometime when I can come home and tell you all about it. I'm having a tough time trying to quit smoking; it costs too much money. It seems to me that I can feel my heart complaining. But I'll have to finish this letter now, because the foreman is waiting to take me with him to town.

My address is c/o Walter Schang, Hussar, Alta.

Love to all from Helge

[*Diary*:] <u>Sat., August 15,1925</u>. Still working for Walter. Today I finished the road work. Am fixing up my binder for the harvest. I think my wages will be $4.50.

<u>Thurs., September 3,1925</u>. Finished the cutting yesterday. We have harvested 2,100 acres. Of those, $640 was for a Mr. Burns. He had a Dane and the Dane's daughter working there. The daughter cooked—she is sixteen years old and is pretty good looking. I had some fun with them, and all the men always talk about Ole and Rosa.

<u>Sun., September 6, 1925</u>. Started threshing last Friday. I am the spike-pitcher and get $1 more a day than the rest of them, but it is terribly hard work.[19]

<u>Sat., September 19, 1925</u>. We are in the middle of the threshing now. We have not done anything since Sunday, September 6. It has rained all the time. To spend the time, I went visiting the neighbour here. His name is Burns, and he is an American. He lives there with his wife and his son by his first wife. They have three men working for them—a German, a Norwegian and a Dane who has a daughter who cooks for him. Lately, I have been over there a lot and had lots of fun with her.

Today I went over to McKinney's, and we had a good time.[20] I played both the violin and the piano. It has been so long since I

[19] Spike pitching was heavy, dirty work—forking bundles from hayracks into the threshing machine, lengthwise, all day, without breaks, except for lunch. Wheat bundles, fully headed, weighed from thirty to thirty-five pounds each, while dust and chaff poured out of the machine, covering the pitcher, getting inside his clothes, his mouth and nose, giving him a thirst he could not quench.

[20] Roy and Leola McKinney moved to Hussar from Palouse, Washington, in 1919, working for Ed Harper until their own place was established.

played the piano that I had almost forgotten how. Frenchy and I went over together and had a ride back. There is a good chess player here, and he and I have had some good games. I made a board out of cardboard, and it works all right. Frenchy does step-dancing. Pete is dancing Russian dances. I play the violin. We all play Whist. Thus we spend the rainy days during threshing time. I had a letter from Alfred about a week ago. He wrote me that I still had 1,280 krone from my inheritance from Aunt Larsen. The money was in the bank.

Tues., September 29, 1925. Snow, snow, snow all over. It is boring me to death. It is still snowing. We have done nothing the last ten days, and even if it does not snow any more, it will be ten more days before it is dry enough. Today I wrote to Corser at Junkins. I am still thinking of working in the forest now and forget about the threshing. Rosa and I have become quite good friends and will correspond this winter. She will go home in about a week.

Sat., October 3, 1925. Snow is still on the ground. But the sun is shining and is quite warm. There is still hope we can do the threshing this fall. All the men quit yesterday. I also figured on quitting. I rode over to Burns's and said a lovely good-bye to Rosa. When I came back, I went in to get my cheque when Walter offered me a job here for $50 a month until we can start threshing again. I accepted. Today I bring straw to the henhouse. All men except Fred (the chore-boy) went to town. I sold my Kodak to Jens for $5 and a double blanket as well. Rosa is leaving on Monday.

Sun., October 4, 1925. Did not do anything today. This morning I was playing with Toots's puppies. They are big now. After dinner, Fred (the half Indian) came back from town. He told me that Big Alex, the Frenchman, still was in Hussar and was drunk as a skunk. Fred brought the mail. There was nothing for me, but quite a bit for Burns, so I brought that over. When I got there, only Ernest was home, and he told me that the rest of them had gone over here. So I rode back again. All of them were here. I then talked to Rosa over here [*at Harper's where father lived*]. They invited me over there to Burns's, but a storm came up, so I stayed at home. After supper, the storm really let loose, and it started snowing. Right now it is snowing for all it's worth. I do not care. I work for monthly wages now and get paid regardless of the weather.

Tues., October 13, 1925. It is clearing now. Several machines have started around Hussar. Walter has still not got any men. Big Alex came back today—broke. He says almost everybody at Hussar is

broke. Rosa went to Medicine Hat yesterday. I am still working for monthly wages. Figured out tonight that I have made $175.
Sat., November 7, 1925. We started threshing October 17 and have since been threshing for seventeen days. I was handy man and spikey [*spike pitcher*]. It has been some tough days. There was snow all over. Since we started, we have only had sunshine one day. I have now made $275. We finished at Walter's and went over to Burns's. Last night we went over to Indian Springs and did four days of threshing. I have received a letter from Rosa and have written her back.
Calgary, November [?], 1925. Now I have been in Calgary for six days. I arrived with $336 and have $100 left. I bought new clothes and have lent Fred Davies $80—helping him to return to New Zealand. The first day I was with Curly and his brother Frank and Gus (the cook). We were at the Grand and saw "Blossom Times," a lovely movie about the life of the composer Franz Schubert. The day after, I bought the music to "Song of Love" and the "Serenade." Curly and his brother left for Ontario Sunday. Monday I met Fred (the New Zealander). He was up against it. He needed $80 for his ticket home. He had no experience in winter work over here and had no clothes. I always liked him, so I lent him $80. So I saw him off.

The next day, I walked up 9th Ave., thinking of meeting Frank Kellow, when I heard some one say, "Hello Nissen." I turned around, and there was Mortensen, assistant at the Danish State Railways. Mortensen, from Ejby, Fyn. I had not seen him for five years. He had left Denmark half a year ago after being fired from the Railways because of a drinking problem. Now he was here in Calgary, broke—no friends or acquaintances. I helped him with some supper and gave him a couple of dollars. He was full of stories about a rich uncle he had in Ontario; and after what he told, he left quite a debt in Denmark, but that is not my business.

First he talked about going to Vancouver, but later he said he was going to Spokane, USA, that same night together with a German "riding the blind" [*riding the rods*].

Another day I walked on 8th Ave., when I happened to look into a cigar store and see John Larsen, whom I was with in Vancouver in 1923. He had travelled around as much as I had since then. We had lots of news to tell each other. His girlfriend in Denmark had broken up with him. He went to Golden, BC, where he had worked the winter before. I have now bought new clothes, hat, scarf, shoes, pen and pencil, music, suitcase, flashlight, underwear, etc. In my haste leaving Walter Schang, I forgot my violin. It was mailed to me. Last Friday I went to a dance at the Scandinavian Club and had a good time. It was a regular "old country" ball.

Calgary, Alta. November 20, 1925
Dear Gudrun & Alfred!

Here I am again. I'm sure you have answered my letter, sent last August, with receipt for my unexpected wealth, but to date I haven't received your letter. I left Walter Schang a week ago, with $336 in my pocket. I now have $100 left, which should prove my talent for getting rid of money when I'm in town. However, please don't get the idea that the money went for booze, cards, etc.—if it had, I probably would not have told you about it.

But I bought myself a good suit of clothes, a hat, shoes, underwear, warm winter clothes and the likes. I also loaned $90 to a friend with whom I worked during harvest, so he will have enough to return to his native New Zealand. He will pay me back next spring. I have also been to the dentist and gave him $45 to work on my teeth. The balance has gone towards minor items, such as a flashlight, scarf, fountain pen, theater, meals and books.

Did I say that I was proud of my talent of getting rid of money? Well now, when the most of it is gone, I feel sort of disgusted! To think that I have worked since last June! Up in the morning 4:30 to 5 o'clock, with hard work all day, to bed at 9 o'clock, never seeing anything but horses and tractors. When I finally get to the city with my friends, it seems natural to feel entitled to enjoy life for a change. Then one by one my friends disappear, and the most of them I will never see again. That's how it goes. It has taken me two years to realize where I stand—it takes the majority of the labour-class a lifetime to realize that there is no future in such a life. I'm almost sick, yearning for a place where I know for sure that I am welcome and needed, where I can have a little music worth listening to! In this country, it is all jazz with a whistling noise. When I once in a while have the opportunity to listen to classical music, there is always bound to be people near me, constantly gabbing away, because they lack the talent for appreciating good music. When I'm out working, it is always: play us a tune, which means "Turkey-in-the Straw," "Red Wing," etc. If I try to play something that I like myself, such as "Ave Maria," they start talking away amongst themselves, and pretty soon I can't hear what I'm playing. So I find it easier to follow the crowd.

But next spring *it will be different,* I promised myself. I'm luckier than the most of them. Though I still have the old habit of leaving my things scattered all over, I get no pleasure out of drinking, playing cards and other temptations open for every young man alone by himself. I am not telling you this just to brag or ease your worries.

I mostly write for the lack of having someone listen to my inmost thoughts with understanding. As far as being liked and needed, there was my New Zealand friend—who got my $90 so he could go back home. He couldn't thank me enough, "I'll never forget you, Chris, and should you ever come to New Zealand, you can always be sure of a home there." I appreciated those words as much as Fred did the $90. On the other hand, take Walter Schang or Frank Corser, two men I worked for. I can always get a job anytime I come there, *but!* if I do *not* get there, they can easily get another man to take my place, and I'm completely forgotten. I'm still thinking about the creamery job. Suppose now that I can get a job at the Viking creamery I told you about last spring. I won't earn half the money, but I will become acquainted around the town of about 1,500 people. The longer I work there, the more experience I'll get, and my wages will increase. After a couple of years, I'll go to school and learn theory; after that the doors should be open for real advancement.

The other day, walking on the street, I heard someone say, "Hello, Nissen." I turned and here it was a former railway man from Fyn, Denmark, who had been fired on account of drinking. He was down and out here for the same reason and was begging for his food—penniless, poorly dressed, unshaven, etc. I had a long chat with him and gave him a few dollars. He wants to go to Spokane in the U.S., with another bum, "riding the blind." I told him he was facing a scary winter and that I spoke from experience. But he would not listen. That is the way it is with drinkers. To think that a few years ago he was my superior, and now he is a beggar on the streets of Calgary. Poor Mortensen!

How is my health? Quite good, though I did have a cold during threshing. They claim that this is the worst fall this country has had since America was discovered. For ten days we threshed in 10 - 20 degrees below zero, with the wind so bad it blew your appendix into a dirigible. There was snow all over, and had been since September 20. I really didn't work very hard, as I had the job of oiling the threshing machine and helping with the tractor, a 75 hp. Caterpillar. During the month of September 3 to October 2, we threshed only ten days. The wheat was too wet the rest of the time. I think I will go back to Frank Corser's tie camps this winter again.

Tell me news from Denmark. I'm not homesick, but long very much for some quiet hours with somebody who cares about me (lonesome, I guess).

Love from Helge

[*Diary*:] Edmonton! November 22, 1925. Well! I am now here; arrived this morning at 8:10. Before I left Calgary, I went into White Lunch and inquired about the chances for a job. At the moment, they had more than enough, but the manager will write when there is an opening. It was a boring trip here. On the way, somebody stole a dollar's worth of magazines. Mrs. Larsen from Hussar left Calgary the same evening as me; she is going to Denmark. Here in Edmonton the first thing I did was look for Actor Huins. I found him after a couple of hours. We did our best to kill time, but time passed slowly. Actor told me that Myrtle Starky had a baby at the end of summer, but it had died about a month later. I took my violin to a violinmaker, and he gave it a general overhauling, and before I took it home, I had spent $12.50—including a new violin case. Will go to Junkins on Wednesday.

Youth Philosophy!

I have now lived in Canada for 2 ½ years. And it has taken me all that time to figure out how things are here in this country. I cannot continue this life much longer; it does not lead anywhere. No matter how good you are driving horses, you will only get $50 per month, and the same goes for the forest in winter. Besides, you travel from one place to another and will never have a home.

No! I will start in a creamery next spring, even if it will cost me ever so much to learn. I am starting to feel so lonesome over here. I do not get to know very many friends, and no *real* friends. Many would call me a big fool loaning Fred the $80 to go some place where he will never see me again. But I was as happy giving him the money as he was receiving it. I knew I would always be able to call him a friend. Today I was stopped by a man who asked for money for supper. I told him he had met the wrong gentleman. He can go to work some place. He had not broken his arm. I long for music and the weaker sex. I long for a home of my own so I do not have to go from one cinema to another to spend time, but I think I will wait until I can get a good Danish girl.

Junkins, Wed., November 25, 1925. Arrived at Junkins at 4 p.m. I met Frank Corser at Swanson's store. We agreed to go out to the camp the same evening. Had supper at Erikson's. At 7 o'clock I met Frank at Herman Johnson's. He had a saddle horse, and I walked beside him the first two miles. When we got to Triggs's, we went in to get a horse Frank had bought there, and I rode it the rest of the way. Arrived at the Camp at 9:30.
Thurs., November 26, 1925. Started working here for $45 per month. Was sent up to Camp 3 to help them at the sawmill for a couple of days. Met old acquaintances from last year: the Borglund boys, Norman and Billy Nielsen.
Sat., November 28, 1925. Finished at the sawmill, and I took a load of lumber back to Camp I.
Mon., November 30, 1925. Started hauling hay.
Thurs., December 3, 1925. Today saw two moose run across the road right in front of me.
Sun., December 27, 1925. Still hauling hay.

1926

Despite another dry year in southern Alberta, agriculture gradually improved. Prices rose dramatically from $1.07 a bushel for Number 1 Northern Wheat in 1923 to $ 1.46 in 1926, and they held at over $1.20 for the rest of the decade.

[*Diary*:] Sun., February 18, 1926. Calgary. Hauled hay for Corser until around February 1. After that, started on ties. I found that way too hard on the horses and quit my job. (He asked horses and men to walk thirty-two miles a day). Got my cheque ($120) and went to Calgary. Have written Walter Schang.
Tues., April 13, 1926. I now work for Walter Schang. We have still not started spring work.
Mon., April 26, 1926. Have started spring work now at Walter Schang's. I am on the Caterpillar outfit. We do not get along here at all. The engineer is so confoundedly smart. He was also here last year, but he behaved much better then. I do not like very many here, and all the work has gone haywire. I came back here thinking that as an old hand at the job maybe I could make a little more, and instead I get more work. I do not like the situation at all.

Sun., May 9, 1926. Am still employed doing spring work. I got tired of working with the engineer. So now I drive eight horses harrowing.

Hussar, Alta., May 10, 1926
Dear Gudrun & Alfred:

It is an awful long time since I wrote you last, and I apologize sincerely. It is time that I tell you a little about my life here in Canada. First I must confess that my ambitious plans about getting into creamery work fizzled out. I was afraid that I would miss the open prairie and freedom. I must admit that I am a little ashamed of myself, but that's how it goes with the young single fellows. I must admit that I'm getting a little homesick. One reason is that the men I work with are always grumbling over the conditions we live under, such as unemployment, the horses we have to work with, the machinery or the bunkhouse where we live. Out here on the farm, it is the poor price of wheat, lack of rain or amusements. Nothing is satisfactory; no one is satisfied the way we are at home. But I don't imagine that there are many opportunities in Denmark either?

At the present, we are busy seeding; we will be finished in a couple of weeks. At present it is raining, and we are laying here in the bunkhouse, doing absolutely nothing. Once in a while, I'll pick up the violin and play a little for my own amusement, but God! I wish I could get together with a piano and play some duets. Or even if I had a good book to read! Here is a run-down of my associates: One Swede age (45), one Dane (47), one Dutchman (46), one Norwegian (40?), one Irishman, one German, one Russian and myself. Well, that should be enough of this kind of gossip?

Last month I bought a Ford, so now have my own car.

Love from Helge

[*Diary*:] August 8, 1926. Still working for Walter Schang. I have driven horses all summer, and soon we are going to start harvesting. All summer I have been busy buying land.[21] I have written home for my own money and tried to borrow $1,000 from Lex; am waiting for Lex's answer.

---

[21] This land was probably in the Wintering Hills. Father does not mention selling it later, but he must have done so—or he may only have been leasing it, as he sometimes confused the terms.

Friends—Chester Thew, who played saxophone in the same orchestra as father, and his brother, Harold Thew, c 1926.

"They All Say I Am Going to Make It" 1927 - 1929

Ole sent this photo of his farm to Emily Petersen in 1929, writing on the back: "Left to right, Prince, Fanny, Pete, Topsy, Scotty, Billy, harrowing! Seeding time, 1929 (in background part of my lake)." Wintering Hills, near Dorothy, Alberta.

1927

Rains returned to southern Alberta in 1927 and provided the first bumper crops since the mammoth harvests of 1915 and 1916 and the strong yield around Hussar in 1923.

[*Diary*:] March 3, 1927. Am still working for Walter Schang. It was a blunder farming on my own. The family would not even help me get my own money, never mind a loan. But maybe it is better that way. Harold Schang is quitting and going back to the U.S. Harper has reclaimed his land, and Walter has now only the two sections of Burns's to farm this year. I have still $400 of last year's wages sitting in his pockets, but believe they are safe. Walter and Harold are going to have a sale in the spring, so they can split their finances between them. Walter is figuring on selling all the old stuff and buying a new Rumely Engine, and then driving it both day and night—he during the day, I, during the night. I have hauled wheat for 4 ½ months this winter and never lost a trip [*overturned a sleigh, spilling the grain*]. At first I had eight horses and two wagons, then we had a heavy snow and we had to use sleighs. We only had six horses then. Around February 10, we (Glen Upstone and I) finished the wheat and drove coal from East Coulee for a little more than a week. Then I stopped driving horses for the winter. I cleaned grain for ten days while Glen drove the wheat for me. Now we are going to put up fence, and we will finish team work for this spring.

I have been to a few dances this winter and had fun. I went to a private birthday party at Martha Wagner's in January. I had quite a bit of fun, though it was something new to me. They played games like we did in Denmark, but we always had to kiss the girls whether I or they wanted it. If just this darned snow could disappear so one could get to town for a dance.

I have not had letters or written home for a dog's age. I wrote a letter to Maren Johanne and one to New Zealand yesterday. Everybody is getting nervous because of what is going on in China, but that does not help any [*Japan had just invaded China*]. If it comes, one man cannot stop the war.

Yesterday I decided to stop smoking; I hope I can keep my promise. I wheeze as soon as I exert myself the least bit. And my heart has started bothering me. I would like to take a trip back to Denmark next winter.

Fri., March 4, 1927. Walter did not get his cook last Wednesday, but the Employment Office agents phoned that she will be on the train today.[22]

Today we started driving ice from Duck Lake. The ice out there is three feet thick. We have a special saw we use for sawing the ice into square pieces. Then we bring it home and pack it into an icehouse together with sawdust. I think it will take four days. Have still not smoked since March 1.

Thurs., March 10, 1927. Have still not smoked, but I am really having a hard time with it. Time flies. We have finished hauling ice and are now working on Walter's McLauglin [*car*]. Have sent an order to Eatons for $33 worth of stuff. Among this, two tires for the Ford. I think I will fix up the old Ford for the summer, though it will cost $100 before it will be all right. Sometimes I think it does not pay to do it. I have to save my money. Walter has not mailed the order yet, so I can cancel it if I feel like.

Fri., March 11, 1927. I managed to cancel the tires from Eatons. We have just had a musical evening, Glen and I. I played 2nd violin and he 1st violin.

Mon., March 14, 1927. Saturday and Sunday the warm chinook wind blew from the south-west and melted all the snow in the yard, and today it snowed another four inches, and it is still snowing. The new cook we got [*Mrs. Innes*] seems to be terribly bored out here. She invited us into the house Sunday, and we played cards all evening with her. Walter sent my order in the mail today. It has been almost two weeks since I smoked my last cigarette. We have given the Buick the first overhaul and are now working on the Dodge truck.

Fri., March 18, 1927. We have now fixed both cars and today started to round up twenty colts which are going to be broken into harness next week. Next Wednesday we shall have an auction here. I have not smoked yet since I quit. This afternoon Walter was at a road meeting and was not at home, so the cook invited us to stay after supper.[23] I danced with her to music from the record player.

---

[22] The Alberta Government refused to put in rural phone lines around Hussar, so, as generally in rural Alberta, the farmers formed their own Mutual Telephone Company, in the mid-1920s. The single wire line, forty miles long and originally held up by 2 x 4s, was built and maintained by the farmers, with the main switchboard in Hussar.

[23] Under the direction of the Local Improvement District, prairie trails were made into roads with fills, ditches and culverts. Meetings would be held to decide which area would get a road next, and those farmers who would help with the work.

She is crazy about dancing. Glen and I do not get along; we argue all the time, so I hope the weather will change soon so we can start the work in the fields. Then there will only be Walter and I. It was far below freezing last night and beastly cold all day. The snow is in huge drifts from the many storms we have had lately.
Sat., March 19, 1927. We were still busy breaking colts today. We, Glen and I, lassoed a big, brown bronco and choked it so it died; it was Glen who did it. When Walter came home and heard that, it was hard on him, and he did not think that it had been necessary to lasso it. It was not my fault it died; I did not have a knife to cut the rope.
Tues., March 22, 1927. We are all busy getting everything ready for the auction over on section 10. This afternoon I was over to oil harness. Today got a letter from Carl Poulsen where he asked me to ask Walter for a job in the spring. Asked Walter but he has no need for him. Rosa, Carl said, is working at the Pottery in Medicine Hat.
Hussar, Sun., March 27, 1927. Walter and Harold had their sale last Thursday. Early in the morning, it was very grey all over, and it looked very dull. Last Wednesday Walter got a telephone message that Harper would be at Hussar the same day, and Walter sent me off to meet them. He phoned in and asked the livery-man to take them as far as he could until they met me. This happened at the Goose Neck Hill. The road was terrible, snow, ice and water.

There were Mr. and Mrs. Harper, Mr. and Mrs. Donovan, Mr. King and Mr. Bell.[24] Everything went all right; I had four horses. It went slow but sure until I came within ¾ mile from home, where there was a big water hole in the road. This I had not noticed before. It was now 9 o'clock in the evening and the horses went straight out into it and were in water chest high. I tried to get them to walk a little more and instead they jack-knifed, and I had to jump into the water to fix them up. I waded in water up to my stomach and got wet through, and cold. We finally got the horses out and cut the fence out and drove around the whole thing. Was home at 10 p.m.

The next day, Harper went over to Walter's sale, but he did not bid on anything, and the stuff was sold awfully cheap. Walter claimed that $5,000 worth of stuff was sold for $2,700. They sold

---

24 Mike Donovan had begun farming five miles northwest of Harper's by 1919. Loretta played the piano and called square dances. Jim King and T. Bell farmed nearby.

everything, so right now Walter does not own a horse or a wagon or anything. On the way home from there (section 10), Harper told me that next year he will parcel out all this land into three farms, and if I wanted, I could rent a section next year. He will divide the 960 acres west of the ranch into two, with one section for Frank's house and a half section with the ranch house. Harper's brother-in-law, Draper, will come up in spring to run this place this summer.[25] He and his wife will move into the ranch house, and Harper and his wife will move into Franky's house. Next year Frank Draper will rent the section that is close to the ranchhouse. Wrote Carl Poulsen yesterday and gave him a quick run-down of the circumstances. I am not too keen getting him up here; perhaps he has a better chance renting Frank Harper's section because he has a big family. Walter will stay here until Harold has left the farm and will then move soon after. There is lots to do here as long as he wants. Glen was sent to town yesterday and returned today and had been stuck for three hours in the same water hole I was last Wednesday. I was sick yesterday and all last night. Had a tremendous nervous headache in the back of my neck; could not lie still. Charley gave me some liniment to drink and I took a couple of doses of salts.[26] I did not eat much supper yesterday. I feel better today, but am not quite all right yet.

Mon., March 28, 1927. Frank Thew bought himself a Case tractor last Saturday.[27] Walter is soon going to Bassano to order his Rumely. Went with a couple of Mennonites over to Section 10 and sold them 200 bushels of oats. We spoke in German, since they hardly knew English. Today we were on the road with a car for the first time this year.

Tues., March 29, 1927. Walter made a valiant attempt at going to Hussar by car, but only got two miles away when he had a blowout and gave up. Very poor road. This evening Martin, Woodford's man (a Dane), was visiting here.[28] Stayed until 10 'o clock. We had quite a good conversation in Danish. Then I played some dances,

---

[25] Frank Draper emigrated from the United States.

[26] Perhaps the salts neutralized the liniment (for external use only) that he drank.

[27] Frank and Amy Thew and family came by car from Garfield, Washington, in May 1919, after buying land next to the McKinneys and Woodfords. Thews worked part-time for the Harpers till their own places were established. Father chummed around with the Thew boys, and would play in an orchestra with Chester.

[28] Luther and Dimple Woodford were brought in by CPR land agents, coming from Seattle, Washington, in fall 1919.

and Glen and Charley danced up a storm. Martin says that Ole's guests are after jobs as cooks in spring. One will have to go up and have a look at them! (Newly arrived Danish girls). Today Charley and Glen started breaking horses. I fixed drills.

Wed., March 30, 1927. Today they again tried to go to town by car and they succeeded. Then Harper took the train to Calgary. Walter and Harold returned, but it was a hard trip. It took them six hours. They were stuck 10 - 15 times. When the cat's away, the mice will play, and after supper Mrs. Innes (the cook) and I danced up a storm to music from the record player. After half an hour, we went out to the bunkhouse and danced to violin music. Both Glen and I played (took turns).

Thurs., March 31, 1927. Today the new cooks arrived (husband and wife who will cook in the field kitchen this summer). They might be Norwegians.

Fri., April 1, 1927. Drove to town today in the middle of a blizzard (sleigh and four horses). When I reached town, the snow had already started thawing again, and when I got one ton of groceries on board, the snow was disappearing at full speed. Harper arrived on the train and was furious that Walter had sent a sleigh instead of a wagon.

Sat., April 2, 1927. I had an awful trip. The snow was almost completely gone. It took me all day to go the twenty miles. When I got to Earl Byrant's, I borrowed his wagon and loaded everything into it.[29] Then I got stuck in a snowdrift and broke the wagon shaft. Roy Minor helped me so I got out around 6 o' clock and went on.[30] Half a mile from home, Walter came to meet me. He drove the team the rest of the way while I took the Dodge home.

Sun., April 3, 1927. This afternoon Mrs. Innes came over to the bunkhouse where we danced up a storm for a couple of hours. Later Walter took her, Glen and me over to Section 10 where Harold Schang held a farewell meeting.

Mon., April 18, 1927. We have now moved over to Walter's own farm—"Peaceful Valley"— he calls it. Walter's Rumely arrived at Hussar last Saturday, and the intention was for us to go in and pick it up. But then it started raining, and we gave up. Now it has been snowing all day. I have worked cleaning up the place. The

---

[29] Earl Bryant and his wife, Barbara, were neighbours.

[30] Minor farmed some land two miles south of father's place, while he lived—and possibly worked—at the Duck Lake ranch, where he was later accidentally killed.

day before yesterday, I received a letter from Maren Johanne [*father's Godmother*]. She gave me a whole lot of Paarup news. All the old acquaintances have married. Walter goes over to Harper's in the morning and does not return until late in the evening. The cook is still here, and she is full of pep. We danced half the day yesterday. There is no music, but that did not make a difference.

Hussar, Alberta, May 3, 1927
Dear Gudrun and Alfred:

I will send you these lines so you know I am still alive. I had a letter from Tage B. [*a family acquaintance*], and he tells me you have sent me letters with your return address and they *never* came back. Well! I have talked to grocer Clifgard, in Hussar, about it (he was postmaster till January 1 this year). He said, of course, the fault wasn't at the Post Office but that so many different people from the country, when they came to town took the mail back with them, and you sort of had to guess who of your neighbours had been in town first that day so you could pick up your mail there. Maybe he is right, but Walter seldom has any trouble with it. Whatever, the Post Office has been moved over to the telephone exchange, and maybe it will be better now. I can assure you I will answer your letters when I get them. I told Tage and will tell you there is *nobody* at home I would rather hear from than *you.*

I was in Calgary the other day and took the opportunity to see a dentist. I had one filling, one crown and a thorough cleaning, and that was all they needed. I had a nasty toothache last summer but didn't take time to see the dentist then, so I was happy to hear that. I also went to a doctor to have my heart examined. I have bit of trouble once in awhile. The doctor said my blood was not good, so he gave me medicine for it. My heart was all right, he said. Sometimes I get an intense heartbeat, especially if my bedroom is too warm, and a couple of times last summer the blood went to my head, and I had a feeling of fainting. I got up and opened the door for some fresh cold air, and it helped. Maybe you should know I live 3,370 feet above sea-level, and many Scandinavians have trouble with their blood for that same reason.

I quit smoking on March 1 and have not yet broken my promise. I have moved over to another place, to Walter's, so now I sleep like a little prince on white sheets. All my clothes get washed for me; everything is up-to-date. Walter's housekeeper has two small children, and they indeed make it lively here. We are not seeding yet—it's raining, snowing and freezing still—and we are getting anxious. Last year we started on April 19. I have now told you about myself. I hope you are well and in good health.

Love to you all from Helge.

Poems

These inclusions in father's diary in 1927 seem to reveal his mind-set, when, with little money, he began farming on his own.

The Undiscouraged Farmer

I met a jolly farmer in a lonely western vale,
A man of fertile fancy that was never known to fail,
Who, when I told of hailstones six ounces full in weight,
Said he had seen twelve-ounce ones back in sixteen sixty-eight.

And when I spoke of fish I'd caught, in certain foreign rills,
that measured twenty-seven feet from narrative to gills,
He said with brow unruffled and manner frank and free,
That he had caught them twice as long in eighteen sixty-three.

And when I spoke of having met a fellow in Berlin
Whose mouth was large enough to get three large potatoes in!
Whereon he wished Jim Hankerson—his cousin—was alive;
He'd seen him hold six apples in his mouth in sixty-five.

It seemed to make no odds to him how I'd exaggerate,
He'd always go one better; so I thought I'd narrate
How with an ass's jawbone did the mighty Samson slay
Ten thousand of his foemen—just to see what he would say.

He listened most intently, with an ever-broadening smile,
As though he were a person who had never heard of guile,
And when I'd done, he told me that he knew the tale was true.
For Samson's self had told it him in eighteen sixty-two.

—Unknown author, newspaper clipping, Meriam, Sask.

The Thrifty Lover and His Love

"I do not need a splendid scene," he said,
"To give me inspiration;
I need no hillside, high and green,
To offer me a glad sensation.
Your presence is enough, my dear,
To make me speak in rhythmic measure,
My soul awakes when you appear,
You fill my heart with priceless pleasure.

"I do not need to travel far
To sharpen my artistic senses;
By finding beauty where you are
I need incur no large expenses.
The sea has grandeur, distant isles
No doubt possess their own attraction,
But I discover in your smiles
A charm that urges me to action.

"The plains of Troy that Helen made
Forever wonderful and thrilling.
The spot where Dido plied her trade
Of blissful cooing and sweet billing —
Those scenes, if it were not for you
Would have a lure that now is lacking
Each day your liveliness I view,
And need no large financial backing.

"How fortunate am I indeed,
You rouse my thoughts to high endeavor,
And sweetly free me of the need
Of any travelling whatever.
It costs me not a precious dime
To gaze upon earth's greatest glory;
Your lightest words are more sublime
By far than any classic story."

She looked far into space, and sighed;
He viewed her with adoring glances.
"I'm sorry," she at length replied,
"To ask concerning your finances,
But if it's not beyond your means
Or counter to your inclination
I'd like a plate of pork and beans
To help to save me from starvation."

—S.E. Kiser (handwritten)

The Limit in Economy

Economy is all very well, but Mrs. Simpkins had got it badly. Her latest stunt was to assemble her eight children and ask them sweetly: "Now, who'll have a penny and go to bed without supper?"

Naturally the youngsters accepted the offer eagerly. Then, in the morning, she would gather them round the table and ask blithely: "Now, who'll give mummy a penny for a nice breakfast?"

—newspaper clipping.

Hussar, June 26, 1927
Dear Gudrun and Alfred!

Thank you for your letter of 29/5. It's a pleasure to hear from you. Yes, I seem to have trouble with my correspondence. It's the same with the friend from New Zealand. I lent him $75 a couple of months ago. I had given up hope of seeing that money again, but I just got a letter for recognition and received the seven pounds [*from Fred Davies, New Zealand*].

I have myself found a nice little "cow-girl" friend, but no engagement yet for the simple reason I don't have anything to get married on, and I won't have until I get started on my own with money I saved up since I first thought of it. I am satisfied here, even if Lex thinks it's the worst climate in the world. I suppose it would be best to start alone without financial assistance, though it's difficult and expensive to buy machinery on credit, but nothing ventured, nothing gained. I understand the money I have at home must wait until I get a little older and go back for a visit, although I could use some here. But remember one thing: just because Lex lives one day of travel closer to Canada than you do, doesn't mean he is closely acquainted with Canada to make sharp remarks. What is there at home that's better? He wants me to try business first. I have started here and am satisfied. There are two groups of farmers. The first one hopes for a million in a short time, and the other group tries to get a comfortable home. The latter are usually into mixed farming—both grain and cattle. They have their own generator for light, a small gas motor to run their pump, churn and washing machine. They have radios and other kinds of music. The taxes are low, so you can see things are fine here, and it's the healthiest place I have lived.

Thank you for your annual report. It's nice to see what's going on at home and see you are doing fine. I am still at Walter's, and here in the area they call me "the working fool." They are all sure I am going to make it. I am very popular with my violin. I don't play for money, but when there are private gatherings, I am invited and asked to bring my violin. That gives me the opportunity to meet a lot of good families. Love to you all.

Yours sincerely, Helge

P.S. I am a Tractor-Engineer this year. I drive the tractor at night.

[*Diary*:] Monday, July 18, 1927. We are busy cultivating section 10 between the rain showers. It is certainly wet here this year. The other day we had a bad hailstorm which completely destroyed Henry Merrit's, Nels Naglorn's, also.[31] Walter had about 10 percent destroyed. It is raining almost every day, and the air is full of electricity with thunder and lightning. There are so many mosquitoes that we have to wear mosquito netting outside, and we cannot sleep at night. I cannot sleep during the day either. Today I slept about three hours, and I have to work all night. This year I finally managed to have contact with somebody who can start me up on a farm of my own, Doc Thompson.[32] He will rent the 320 acres west of the Allan section to me. He has plowed all summer and is running short of money. We have arranged it so that I, for last year's wages, will get Walter to break 75 to 100 acres and Doc will break 75 acres. I will get the crop as security. Next year I will put in the crop, and after that run Doc's Rumely.

Hussar, November 16, 1927. Have now got time for the diary again. I have worked hard this summer. Now the snow is two feet deep, and I am resting these days. Walter bought himself a tractor binder with a special engine-drive attachment. So we harvested section 16 with the Rumely and a ten foot binder. I was the engineer most of the time, and Bud assisted me. When the grain was harvested, Walter bought a twenty-eight inch Minneapolis separator and threshed for Billy Treend and let his own field wait.[33] The result

---

[31] The Henry Merrit family, with their four pretty daughters, were among the earliest settlers in the area, living near Harpers. Nagloren was a bachelor who had come to the Duck or Sieu Lake district from Norway, via the USA, in 1922.

[32] Doc Thompson—apparently not a physician—travelled in the States, selling land for the CPR, and, at Hussar, drove landseekers to their prospective sites. Farming west of father was a Mrs. D. L. Thompson, perhaps a relative of Doc's.

[33] Billy Treend's father, W. R. Treend, moved from Saskatchewan in 1901 to the Wintering Hills where the family ran one of the huge early ranches. In 1927 he also owned land adjacent to Schang's. Billy and his wife, Mae, farmed in the Indian Springs district.

was that he was caught in a snowstorm, and now we will have to wait till spring before we can thresh again. I did not have time to plow that half section west of the Allan section, but now I have rented a whole section east of the Allan section. The land belongs to a man by the name of Worley (a cousin of Thompson's). I have to arrange it with Doc so that I can use his tractor for seeding next spring. Wrote him a letter yesterday. Walter bought a GMC truck (1½ tons), and I have been busy hauling wheat to town.

Ole Nissen, left, operating a Holt "Combined Harvester." Man on right unknown, possibly Glen Upstone. Schang outfit, near Dorothy, 1920s.

1928

The tremendous soil moisture carry-over from 1927 ensured that crops in 1928 would again be bountiful. Around Hussar, frost damaged the grade, but the spirit of farmers remained positive and optimistic.

Hussar, Alta., January 2, 1928
Dear Alfred!

Thanks a lot for your kind Christmas letter. I'm sorry that I didn't manage to send a Christmas letter to you this year. With regard to "Bikuben" [*Danish Bank*], I hope that this matter [*re the inheritance*] will be settled before spring because I did write to them for a receipt blank.

Thanks a lot for the book. There are many good things in it. But there are also many things that would make you smile if you lived over here. What he says about Danes who live among Canadians is much exaggerated. And at the same time, I know that the Danes in the Standard colony can quarrel & disagree. And you must not think that Canada wishes to have another Tower of Babel either. They all turn up their noses at Danes who go to the colonies & don't bother to learn the English language.

Yes, I have got a farm for myself and must seed 200 acres next spring. I have a contract for three years tenancy. The winter is *hard*. Worse than they have seen for many years. *Snow, snow,* and then there are so many blizzards, which come out on the middle of the prairie so you can't see three feet in front of you. I have been caught by surprise a couple of times already and have a couple of frozen ears and a frozen nose as a souvenir. I'm playing violin in the Hussar orchestra and manage fine.[34] On the 11th of this month, I'm going to play solo for a theatre audience ("Souvenir," "Ave Maria" and "Angel's Serenade"). If I get a good harvest next year, I'll come home next winter!

I'm in the best of health; my teeth are in #1 condition. Next summer for sure, I'll get myself photographed and send you a picture. The point is, I don't like to show my face more than necessary, because I look so old. These winters have been hard on me, because I have not had enough sense to stay inside and care for my face. And my nose is spoiled quite a lot since I was kicked by

---

[34] This was Dorothy Reesor's orchestra. She and her husband lived in Hussar from the spring of 1925 to 1929. Dorothy later wrote: "I had a good orchestra consisting of Ole Nissen, a Danish young man, who played so well, Dutch Bryant and Manville Anderson on sax, and Romeo Brassard on drums. We really had some wonderful dances and concerts in the new community hall, and we also went to play at Standard, Chancellor and Meadowbrook Hall. When we went to play at Standard we would travel up the railroad on the speeder.... It was a mighty cold ride, but I think it was better than getting stuck in the mud and gumbo as it was then. I remember going to play at Makepeace in the winter and we all piled into a sleigh. On the way home in the wee small hours, one of the horses dropped dead, and we had to walk about three miles to get home. Yes, many a cold night we set out for Wintering Hills, and all those places, but it was fun and a rich experience which I enjoyed." —The Hussar Historical Society, *Hussar Heritage*, p. 221.

a horse in 1924. But that's all right, and I would be glad if only I could see you all again.

Now, love and Happy New Year's wishes to you all,

from Helge

[*Diary*:] Hussar, January 8, 1928. Time flies. Now we are in the middle of winter, and I cannot understand how time flies.

In the month of December, I have hauled wheat for Roy McKinney and withstood some bad snowstorms. This has been the hardest winter Alberta has experienced for a long time. Throughout the winter, I have been playing in the Hussar orchestra and have had many enjoyable hours, and also made lots of extra pocket money.[35] On the 11th of this month, I am going to play for the theatre production at Hussar.

My cashbook is doing quite all right. I have $841 from Walter and $50 from McKinney. I have started keeping a cashbook again. My plan for next year is to hire Walter to seed my crop and work for him next summer. Today I bought a team of horses from Shay Vermilion.[36]

Sat., January 14, 1927. Well! Now the theatre production is over and done with, and it went well. They applauded me and asked for an encore after I had played "Traumeri," and then I played "Angel's Serenade." Also the dance afterwards went well. The Ladies' Aid had a $200 profit. But the work of the orchestra was all charity, so all I had were quite a few expenses from it. I arrived Monday and stayed until Thursday morning, and that cost me $15. Well, I had a good time anyway.

Today Walter went to Calgary; he had some business to do. He is working on a truck which can haul wheat in snow by the help of a rubber crawler belt. I have my horses in Walter's barn and have driven them several times and like them well. These days I am

---

[35] Romeo Brassard, who played drums, came with his parents, Henry and Lucienne Brassard, from Massachusetts, in 1916. They had sold a prosperous business after a CPR agent told of the fortunes that awaited them in Alberta. Farming southwest of Hussar, they soon lost everything to drought, moved to Vancouver, then returned to Hussar where Henry worked for wages at various jobs. Romeo left Hussar in 1930 to work at a machinery agency and as an electrician, at Sylvan Lake.

[36] Shay and Grace Vermilion and sons came from Palouse, Washington, in 1920, to Carmangay, Alberta, then to the Wintering Hills, and finally to the Duck Lake area—about six miles southwest of father's place—in early 1927, where they farmed and ranched.

thinking of buying another team so I can have four horses this summer and next harvest. Walt has figured out how much I have made the last couple of years, and the result was that he owes me $841. So I think I shall weather the storm.
Sun., January 22, 1928. Last Friday I went to Hussar; I took four horses and bundles of wheat for feed. The same evening, I drove with a bunch of Hussar people to Makepiece to play at a dance there together with Mrs. Reesor. We had a good program and made $6 apiece. At the same time, we had an order to play at a dance at Standard on Friday, January 27. We returned to Hussar at 5 in the morning. At 8 o'clock I drove home with a load of fence posts (200) for Worley. It tipped over twice, and Ed Wall helped me reload; but the second time we let half of it lie down at Jim King's east-field, approximately eight miles from here, so I will have to go to get them tomorrow. I have hauled 290 fence posts out.
February 4, 1928. Am now hauling wheat for Walt. The weather is quite good. Today I had a letter from Clara Roed [*former girlfriend in Denmark*]. She is still a Miss, and sent a nice letter. On Friday, January 27, I was at Standard and played at a dance and had a good time. At the end, I played some Danish dance tunes, and they could hardly stop applauding. We went there in a one-horse carriage, and on the way home I was almost run over.

Hussar, February 17, 1928
Dear Brother [*Alfred*]!

I hope you received my New Year's letter. Everything is fine as usual. I delivered wheat almost the whole winter and have at the moment $900, and furthermore, I've bought a team of horses. But the entire earnings will be spent this summer until I get my first harvest in the fall. It's natural that you, who have taken care of my affairs so far, are interested in how I stand. I have leased a section of land (640 acres of land) of which 200 acres is ploughed & ready to seed. The lease is for three years. This summer he (the owner) will plough 120 acres more, which gives me 320 acres to seed next year. In Canada they take two harvests from the same field before it's plowed again; thereafter it's plowed every second year. (One year grain is grown, and the next year none is).

For the moment, there is only one granary on the land. My plan is to stay at Walter's this summer, and as soon as my land is ready to be seeded in the spring, I'll hire him to seed it for me. The owner will pay for half of the seed, & I will pay for the other half.

This will cost me about $130. Then I will stay at Walter's this summer and earn $75 a month. When it's harvest time, I'll move to my own land, harvest, and combine my profits. Meanwhile, I have to do my own cooking and live in the granary. When the time comes, I will have Walter or anyone else who comes first, to thresh the grain for me, and I'll drive it to the railway myself. That will be only three miles, as they have worked all winter on a new railway, which is rather close to my land. It would take me the whole night to give you enough details for you to be sufficiently informed, but I can tell you, that if I get 25 bushels to the acre this year, I will earn more than $2,000, and here 25 bushels to the acre is normal. But to do the harvesting, I will have to buy four horses and a binder; four horses and harness cost $350, and a binder costs $285. After threshing, I also have to buy a buggy which will cost $275. So it costs money to start farming. But then I will have every thing for next year. After the harvest, the owner intends to build a house and a barn and dig a well.

Love to Gudrun and the children from your devoted

Helge

P.S. Please excuse my haste, but it's 8 p.m., and I must get up at 3 a.m. tomorrow morning to drive a load of grain to town (twenty-five miles). Because it thaws so badly during the day and since there was so much snow this winter, the sleigh may fall through and then turn over—so I start as early as possible in the morning before the sun melts the snow again. (It freezes at night).

[*Diary*:] Mon., February 20, 1928. Today Walter and I went for a ride in Walter's GMC truck for the first time this year. After the thaw we have had for a while, enough snow had gone so we could "circle" around the snowdrifts. We started for East Coulee coal mine, and I sat at the wheel. We made good progress until we reached the top of East Coulee hill where we had an accident which almost cost us our lives. I rounded a curve, and the road was full of ice, and before we knew it, the rear end started sliding, and before we knew that we were over the bank. We fell down more than 100 feet, almost straight down. The only thing that helped us was that the rear end slid first, and that made the truck go down straight, the rear end first. The other thing which helped us was a group of trees on the bank. We smashed into them, and they broke like matchsticks, and we were more than 100 feet down before we stopped. If the trees had not been there, or we had slid over sideways, it would have been the end of us. Now we had a road between the trees, and I went over to the Griffins, three miles, and got them to come with four horses, and after three hours' work, we finally got the truck up again. We then drove back to the top and drove home again.

Tuesday the 14th of this month, Manville, Carl [*Jones?*] and I were at Chancellor to play for a Valentine's Dance and had a good trip. I had all the fence posts out and got my $20 from Worley. On Wednesday, I am going to Hussar to play for a dance there. Today wrote a letter to Clara.

Wed., February 29, 1928. Today went to a Leap Year dance at Hussar, and I had a terrific time. I drove in with Lyle [*Tonneson*] and in Hussar got the big surprise to be invited to the dance by Gladys Thew. It was "Ladies' choice" until 12 o'clock, and I did not sit one dance out; at 12 o'clock Gladys and I went for supper, and she paid (according to the rules). After 12, I paid all my dances back and had a great time. I played a couple of square dances and schottishes, etc., to relieve the school band. Today I had a letter from Rosa Poulsen, Alfred, and Maren Johanne.

Thurs., March 1, 1928. Worked on the Rumely. Last night I went over to the Bryants' and arranged things with Ed Wall so we could go to the dance at Wintering Hills tomorrow. At the same time, I saw Nat Bryant and got him to write to Kimbrough about the quarter section west of my place; I wanted to buy it on "crop payment."[37] At the same time, he tried to get me to join the Wheat Pool.[38]

Sat., March 3, 1928. Today went to a dance at Wintering Hills. Went together with Ed Wall. I rode over to the Bryants' at 7:30. When I got there, I saw Ed in the house with his work clothes on. Gladys Thew was over there, and Ed did not like to go without her, but he had not shod the horses. I phoned Frank Thew, but he would not let her go. So I finally got Ed to go, anyway. We reached the school at 11 o'clock. There was a good crowd, and they had just started.

---

[37] Crop payment: some or all of the profit from each crop would go to Kimbrough until the land was paid for.

[38] The Alberta Wheat Pool was incorporated in 1923. Farmers, dissatisfied with the grain marketing conditions in the West, organized a drive, signing up 50 percent of the 1922 wheat acreage for the new Pool. A Pool office was opened in Calgary. In 1925 three Pool elevators were built—Hussar's opened the next year, and soon they were in every grain-shipping point in Alberta, with the farmers sharing the profits. —The Hussar Historical Society, *The Hussar Heritage*, p. 48.

When I came in, they were playing records. Before I went in, I had a drink of wine from Bob Halsey. I danced the first dance with Zona Bell.[39]

Then I took out my violin and played a square dance together with Louis Hoeght & Chester who were both there. I had a few pieces of music with me. Then I got Zona to play with me. I had a great time. Zona was beginning to warm up to me. I asked her to come to the dance the next Friday, but since it was so far away, it would be quite difficult for me to come and pick her up. She said that she understood that all right. Jack Zerky was at the dance. He gave me a swig of wine and gin.

Sun., March 4, 1928. Came home from the dance at 6 a.m. Slept until 1 o'clock.

Hussar, March 4, 1928
Dear Alfred!

Thank you for the letter (February 7) which I received a couple of days ago. You really asked me a lot of questions this time. Part of them, I believe I've already answered in my earlier letter. My share of the seed is 95 bushels of wheat (about $100) and 25 bushels of oats ($12). His (the owner's) share is 110 bushels of wheat.

All there is on the place at the moment is a granary (14 x 16 feet). But the conditions of the lease are that he will build a house and barn and dig a well. The ground has never been cultivated before last summer, when Worley (the owner) hired a tractor to plow ("break," as they call the first plowing) 200 acres. It's all prairie land. I have bought three horses so far—($160) and two sets of harness ($100), and I'm watching out for a fourth horse. They are all young horses, and everyone praises me for my good buy.

While I was delivering wheat this winter, I carried a few fence posts home with me each trip for my fence next year. For fencing over here, we use barbed wire stretched up over a row of cedar posts, three wires. It takes 320 posts for a mile, and I have to build 1½ miles in the spring. I received $20 to bring the posts out, and it didn't cost me a cent. I get $60 to build the fence, and it will take me about a week. The lease is for three years. The owner will pay for half the seed and half of the threshing expenses and gets half

---

[39] Zona Bell lived in Hussar. Her father was a hardware store manager—later owner—and her mother was active in the community.

of the (harvested) wheat. Against this, I must do the harvest and deliver it to the railway which will be about three miles from my land. This year he will hire the same man to break another 120 acres and also do the discing and harrowing so it will be ready for seeding next year. Since it's necessary to use the land for two years after it is broken, I must seed the same 200 acres next year, and that will give me 320 acres. The land is not a paradise to work with because it's rather rolling and has some sloughs, but it's a good chance for me to start up cheaply. If I'm not satisfied, I can always give it up after three years.

Dear Alfred, I'm now going to ask you to do me a great service. Try to get the following music for me: 1) The Hungarian Dances, exactly like you have them at home; 2) Goldermann's Romances, also like your own; 3) Other good duets for piano and violin, which are not too difficult to play. You know my taste, it's nearly the same as your own. And this is why: Canada and USA's music is mostly jazz. If you want some good pieces, these are only for artists. On the 14th of this month, I'm going to play some solos in Hussar. As we didn't know what to choose (we have almost no music), we got our hands on F. Drdla's "Souvenir" and a few more, and then we sent for the Hungarian Dances. We got one dance, "No 5," but it was revised for a virtuoso and had almost all double grips which I could not even start to play.[40] Then I got angry and told them that I would send to a country where you could get some pieces that an ordinary man could play. You would give me great pleasure if you could arrange this for me. I don't know how much it costs but hope you can get the money from my account in the bank.

My frozen ears & nose are better now & forgotten. The worse that happened was the skin came off and new skin grew out again. You talk about my clothing. Maybe it would interest you to get a description of my clothing when when I deliver wheat. First of all, imagine a grain box on sleigh runners, six horses (2 + 2 + 2) in front of you, and twenty-five miles of ceaseless up and down hills, and minus 20 F., and the wind thirty miles per hour from the northwest. I have next to me two wool underwear (vests and trousers in one) one wool shirt & wool trousers. Then overalls, leather vest, wool windbreaker (thick) and a fur coat with a big collar,

[40] Double grips consist of drawing the bow over two strings at once. Father could play these, of course, but on a simpler level.

which reaches over my head. On my feet, I have two pairs of wool socks, one pair of high boots, one pair of USA overshoes. On my hands, a pair of thick woolen mitts and a pair of thick deerskin over mitts. Then I shouldn't freeze, but the wind goes through everything.

On my head, I have an ordinary cap with earflaps. But I get frozen in a blizzard. These come very often without warning—and you can't see five feet in front of you. No matter if you walk with the wind—the snow blows from the ground right up in your face. The snow sticks to your face, thaws and freezes before it drops off. And then you have to use your fingers to scratch the ice away. Especially on your eyelids! The snow melts on them and freezes to ice, and before you know it, you can't see. Then you have to take off your mitts and scratch it off, and this is cold on the fingers. I was out in a blizzard for two hours this winter (two weeks before Christmas). I was two miles from a farm when the storm came and had a hard time making my way to it.

I'm sorry to hear about your fall, but I hope you are better now. I nearly had an accident last month. We had a thaw for awhile and most of the snow had disappeared, so Walter and I went in his truck down to a coal mine by the Red Deer River about eight miles from here—I drove it. The last two miles was a steep hill down to the river. We had just begun to go down the hill on which was a very steep grade, when the rear wheels slid on the ice, and before we knew it, we went (fortunately) backwards down the slope. There was 150 feet of an almost perpendicular angle and then a step and then a 300 foot drop. Fortunately, the first slope had trees growing on it and these broke like matches, but they slowed us down, so we didn't slide out over the drop. Everyone who has seen the place can't understand how we did it.

We got the truck up again at another place, with horses, and *drove home.*

Now I have to close, and I'm sending you all my love and wish you happiness and blessings.

from Helge

[*Diary*:] Thurs., March 8, 1928. It is bone cold these days, and we are not doing much. Today I wrote a letter to Maren Johanne. Last Saturday, I wrote Alfred. We play cards every evening. I have still not bought seed wheat and do not know where to buy it. But I have an idea that I will buy some good wheat in Edmonton and most of the seed wheat from Robinson and the oats from Bunney.[41] Tomorrow I am going to Hussar, and I will stop at Wintering Hills School and go to the UFA dance. Last Saturday I joined the Alberta Wheat Pool.

Wed., March 14, 1928. Today was the big day at Hussar. I took Pete & Topsy and drove to Hoeght's where I stopped and took the whole family with me to town.[42] The play started at 8 o'clock and everything went smoothly; I played a couple of solos, "Souvenir" & "Intermezzo" from Il Travatore. Everybody had fun. I drove the Hoeghts back and slept there. Went to bed at 6 a.m. Made $3.50.

Fri., March 16, 1928. Was at a dance at Chancellor and made $8. The dance was good, but I had a bad cold.

Sun., March 20, 1928. Went on a saddle horse to Stony Ridge and looked over the place. It looks good enough to me. Ed and Benny Wall went with me. After that we went down to Dorothy [*twenty miles southeast of Drumheller*]. Jerry and I tried to go along the river up to where they work on the railroad, but were stopped by water & ice because the river is ready to break up. Then we turned around again and rode up to old Ross and stayed there for supper.[43]

Tues., March 22, 1928. Today Walter came home from Calgary. I drove over to Sam Clifgard's to get him, and on the way home, I bought a horse from Earl Bryant for $60.

Wed., March 23, 1928. Today I went to an auction at Griffin's and bought a horse there for $37. It is nine years old. It is a roan and looks quite good; hope it is not balky. Today wrote a letter to Doc Thompson and asked about written permission to get Worley part of the wheat.

Tues., March 27, 1928. Today had a letter from "Bikuben"; they will send me my money through the mail. Yesterday I bought 100 bushels of wheat from Paul Noiser ($105). I have also picked up the horse I bought from Earl Byrant. So now I have four horses.

---

[41] Bryce H. Bunney came from England via Guelph, Ontario, in 1891, working on large ranches in southern Alberta. He was in charge of a trainload of cattle on one of the first trains to cross the Crowsnest Pass. After fighting in the Boer War, he established a ranch west of father's place, specializing in Percheron horses. He and his Australian-born wife had a daughter, Isobel, who later married a Mountie. The Roy Robinsons lived immediately west of the Bunneys.

[42] This was the family of Louis Hoeght with whom father played in the orchestra.

[43] Louis H. Ross, a bachelor, farmed a few miles north of father's place. He liked to ride horseback into Dorothy, spending hours visiting in the store with Russell Kidd.

Fri., March 30, 1928. I was at Standard and played for an amateur play and a dance. Had quite a good time and made $6. But I lost both my own money and Dutch's, so that was the end of that fun.
April 11, 1928. Yesterday I had two letters from Clara. I was really happy and answered her today. Also received letters from Doc Thompson and Worley and answered them. Fatty, the horse I bought from Earl Bryant, foaled the other day, but we had to help her with it and the colt was dead. She is now sick, and we do not know if she will survive.
May 27, 1928. Well, now the spring rush is over. I finished seeding May 3, and Walter finished threshing yesterday. I haul wheat to town by truck, four trips a day, 180 miles a day. Today I signed a life insurance for $3,000 with Monarch Life Co.
July 6, 1928. It is the same kind of weather this year as last year, and the wheat looks good. A couple of days ago, I received a letter from Clara [*Roed, in Denmark*], and she says that she loves me. I wonder how much. I doubt she loves me enough to come over here? I insured for hail about a week ago ($1,080). Today Walter and I figured out how much he owes me, and we arrived at $615. Worley and his family were here the other day and stayed for a couple of hours. It does not look as if I will get a house there.
Sat., July 7, 1928. The rain stopped last night, and we started plowing with the horses this morning.[44] I ground valves on the Rumely. Last night, Ed Wall was over visiting me, and we talked about Clara. He stayed for so long that he ended up staying over night and slept with me. He is crazy about going to Denmark with me. Topsy [*the horse*] is sick these days. She has boils all over her body. At 8 p.m. I started plowing with the Rumely tractor and managed to get soaking wet; went home at 2:30 a.m.
July 8, 1928. Got up at 7 a.m., went out to the plow and got the men started. Then went home and changed clothes. After dinner, I went over to the Bunneys' in the GMC. Played together with Mrs. Bunney and Isobel. Left at 7 p.m. On the way home, I looked at the wheat, and it looked fine. One mile from the house I went into a hole filled with water and was stuck. It was raining. I ran home. It was only a shower. Went into the fields at 9 p.m. and

---

44 They may have been summerfallowing or plowing on father's farm. On February 17, father wrote that "this summer" Worley, the owner, who hired his work done, would break 120 more acres. This plowing began just after Worley's visit.

plowed with the tractor. From 10 p.m., a large thundercloud was hanging over me, and there was constant lightning, but it did not rain, so I had to continue. Worked there all night.

July 9, 1928. At 7 a.m. the day workers came, and I got them started. Then Walter and I went up to the water hole where I was stuck with the car and worked there until noon but could not get it out. Went to bed at 1 p.m. and got up at 6:30 p.m. Drove the tractor until 1:30 a.m. when I was surprised by a violent thunderstorm. Went to bed at 3 a.m.

July 10, 1928. Got up at 7. Helped Fred [*Schang's hired man*] catch the nine horses and hitch them up. Went home. Worked on the truck. After dinner, I drove over to Thew's and loaded sixty bushels of wheat and drove to town. Terrible roads. Mud up to one's ears. Drove back to the Thew's. Had supper and then drove out and loaded seventy-five bushels wheat, and when I started the load, I broke a rear axle. Went with Chester down to get the Thew's tractor which took the load away from the granary. Then worked on the truck until 12 midnight. Then drove with Chester home to Walter and had him have a look at it. Walter and I came home at 2:30 a.m. After that, I went out and drove the tractor (Rumely) until 7 a.m. Went to bed at 8 a.m.

July 11, 1928. Slept until 2 p.m. Rode the saddle horse over to Stony Ridge to look at my wheat. It looks quite good, but is rather "spotted" [*unevenly germinated*]. Fifty percent is headed. After that I rode over to the Bunneys' and invited Isobel to a picnic. She can go, but I have to take Mrs. Bunney in the bargain! Then rode home and started plowing at 8 p.m. Plowed until 12 midnight and stripped two gears. Then I walked home and got hold of Walter, and we worked there until morning. Now we have stopped for a couple of days. Went to bed at 8:30 a.m.

Hussar, November 13, 1928

Dear Gudrun and Alfred,

Thank you very much for your letter and the pictures; it was really nice to hear from home again. Yes! I know darn well it's my fault, but now the hurry is over for this time so I have to let you know how I am.

I had a good harvest, but the frost came early & damaged my wheat a lot. Although I must not complain—I made much more money than if I had worked for wages. But the money goes to more horses and machinery and housekeeping. I also made good pocket money by playing at dances (balls, I mean), and the notes you sent me were a great success, apropos! Alfred asks me if I got them—we don't use the Hungarian Dances for American jazz dances, but sometimes when they have a particularly fine movie, they send for the pianist and me, and then we play all the old pieces. It's all so primitive over here that the movie theatre here is as important as the Royal Theatre in Copenhagen.

It was my intention to come home this winter, but I'm sorry that it's not possible now. First I wasn't able to deliver my wheat to town, because the elevators are always full. A lot of trucks were sold in Canada this year, and these trucks are driving the wheat in so fast that the railway can't ship the wheat away fast enough. And the result is that it all stops. And we small farmers with horses and sleighs have no chance at all. But when the snow begins falling, the trucks must stop, and then I can get my 5,000 bushels delivered.

A "new modern truck," heavy duty, possibly an International, Nat Bryant's, late 1920s. Trucks began appearing on the prairies after WWI, with Frank Thew buying a six-wheeled semi-truck in 1925, first in the area.

And secondly, I have a plan to go home next winter and bring with me a sweet little "Mrs. Nissen" so that she can meet my family and you can meet her. Her parents are Danes, but she doesn't speak much Danish herself. Her parents came to the States when they were very young, and after they had children who went to

English speaking schools, then Danish was no longer spoken at home. They are now living in Standard and are wealthy. Of course, it's too early to say for certain, but it would be my greatest wish. Her name is Emily Petersen, and she is 20½ years old. She doesn't play piano, but is still musical, and who knows? Maybe she can learn it.

Emily Petersen, 1927 or 1928.

I'm only four miles from the new railway that was built this summer by the Red Deer River; in a month or so, it will open up [*for service*], and then I can deliver my wheat there. This means a difference of twenty-two miles to me!! It has been very dry this fall, and there have been a lot of prairie fires, but none around where I live. My house is not yet a castle, but it's my own. I don't have a barn yet for my horses, but I'm beginning to build it next week. There will be a terrible situation next winter, especially if times get hard.

There were so many workers for the threshing season that they didn't make much money, and now they walk around town. Every day you read in the newspapers about robberies and sometimes even murder.[45] How will it be when winter comes? Is it the same at home? Gudrun asks if I have a car? Yes, I have an old Ford car. It's all I can manage yet.

---

[45] The year 1928 brought a bumper crop to the prairies. To help with the harvest, over 8,000 men were brought over from Britain, where there were over a million unemployed. Out on the prairies, most of the men adjusted well, but with others, problems arose. Inexperienced and unused to physical labour, they quickly became unhappy. Many of these men gathered in the nearest towns and cities where disturbances occurred daily. After harvest, over 6,000 of the men were transported back to Britain; the rest were absorbed into bush camps, railways, mines and cities.

It's nice to hear that you are all well. Even if you get some hard knocks now and then, it teaches us to enjoy life. I feel a little lonesome these days because I have been out threshing all fall (and earned good money), and I'm quite alone. But I've enough to do, so that's OK. I intend to buy a radio this winter. Well! Now I have to get myself some supper, so I'll close for this time with love to you from

Yours, Helge

P.S. It was quite funny to see you calling me Helge! Over here they never call me anything besides "Ole"!

[*Diary*:] November 20, 1928. Much has happened since July, and I am sorry that I have not written in my diary. I bought myself a batching outfit and lived on my own farm [*on Stony Ridge*] while I harvested my own crop. I had three men stooking for me. After the harvest, I hired out with Walter's thresher, and we started out threshing my crop. All together I had 4,800 bushels. After the threshing, I moved home again and now live at home.

Ole Nissen's tarpaper shack on Stony Ridge, Wintering Hills, near Dorothy, 1928 or 1929.

Hussar, December 10, 1928
Dear Gudrun and Alfred,

I'm afraid that it's soon Christmas, and now you will not get this before it's over, but I'll hope you'll forgive me, and I think it's

Ole's granaries, 1928 or 1929. Beyond is unsold CPR land which Ole had to fence to keep out range horses.

better late than never. Yes, the time is going so fast over here. When I began working this spring, I was delighted, thinking how happy I would be when I could buy horses that I could call my own. But as time went by, I forgot all about it. I earned some money this year, but the frost destroyed my wheat so that it was worth only three-fifths of the price I could have had if nothing had gone wrong. I'd like you both to come out here to my farm and take a look at it all (it's not so much). You would enjoy the sight. I live in a house measuring 14 x 16 feet. Here I sleep, do my own cooking, settle my accounts, play the violin and all.

Because of the new modern trucks which have come to the prairies it's hard for those without them to get rid of grain, but now the worst time is over, and us little farmers can start to deliver grain. I live only twenty-six miles from Hussar! You can figure out yourself the distance in Danish. It would be a long way when you have 3,200 bushels to deliver (I've already driven 1,600 bushels in) and only 125 bushels every second day. But we have got a new railway down by the Red Deer River, and it's only four miles from my farm, and that's where I'm delivering my wheat this year. To get down to the railway (it follows the river all the way, on the other side), you have to go down a long steep hill. The way it twists and turns, it's very dangerous to use when it snows or rains. The railway has just started and won't take passengers for another half year. The Government of Alberta hadn't budgeted for it this year. It would have been impossible to drive the wheat down the hill, so we all got together and laid a pipeline down the hill, from top to bottom.[46] Now we drive our wheat up to the slope and let it run through the pipeline. Below, there is a truck that drives it over the frozen river to the grain elevators.

My violin gives me many happy hours. I'm the only one in Hussar who can play the violin, so you can see what chances this gives me—now, in these winter evenings I've many free hours, and I've transposed most of the Romances and Nocturnes to the violin.[47] Three miles from me, there is a horse rancher by the name of B. Bunney, and his wife plays the piano very well, and we have many good hours. We're now playing all of the Hungarians.

I'm spending Christmas in Standard at the Petersens' this year. I think I told you about Emily in my last letter. She has been ill for the last month and has not yet recovered. Inflammation in the ears—dangerous—but the doctor thinks that she'll be able to hear well again. Next Christmas I hope you'll have us both with you. It's the idea now at least.

I now have ten horses, harness, buggies, plough, sawmill, etc.; most are paid for. I have a $70 kitchen range and up-to-date cooking equipment. Then I have $400 more owing to me by Walter Schang, which he can't pay me right now. So far we have had the mildest winter Alberta has seen for many years, almost no snow, and we're walking outside in shirt sleeves on Dec. 10. It's almost impossible to believe.

I'm enjoying splendid health and was in Calgary a month ago

---

[46] Building the chute were Earl Bryant and Ed Harper, with neighbours helping to lay the six inch metal pipe which extended some 300 feet to the bottom of the steep hill. At the top, farmers unloaded their trucks into a sloping trough that funnelled the grain down the chute into an overhead bin located at the bottom, from where it was loaded into a truck and carried across the frozen river to the grain elevators a mile away. It was much needed during the 1928 season, as the Bryants sold 100,000 bushels of grain, and the Harpers, 60,000 bushels. The next year a graded road was built down to the ferry, eliminating need for a chute. —Hazel Roen, *The Grass Roots of Dorothy* (Calgary: Northwest Printing and Lithographing, Ltd., 1980), p. 174.

[47] There were others in the area who played the violin at dances, such as Clarence Harmer and Bert (Shorty) Westover—but perhaps father was referring to his classical training.

for my annual dental check-up. This summer I took out a $3,000 life insurance, so everything is in fine shape. I have a barn for ten horses and lots of feed, and I'm in every way satisfied with the world. So now let me hope that you can send me a letter back just as quickly.

A sincere wish for a good and happy New Year to you all from

Helge,

your brother-in-law, brother and uncle, in a foreign land.

[*Diary*:] After Christmas, 1928.

Emmie

It was at a dance at Chancellor in August, I first met Emmie! I played with the Hussar band, and then I saw her. I kept trying to establish eye contact, and finally got a smile from her. Later in the evening, I did not play one dance and walked up to her and introduced myself. She gave me her name, Emily Petersen, and I danced that dance with her. She came to the following dances at Chancellor and Standard, and I kept dancing with her whenever I had a chance. I learned that it was her father's hired hand, Matt, who took her to the dances, and that she did not particularly like him, but I had a tough time pushing him out. I started corresponding with her, and during threshing time I finally managed to take her to a dance. I borrowed Walter's Buick and had some wonderful days with her.

In December she got sick and had to go to Calgary to see the doctor. She had terrible pains in her ear and nose. She stayed there until Christmas, and I went in to see her twice during that time. She wrote me every day, and I answered her almost as often. At Christmas I was invited out to her home at Chancellor [*Standard was their hometown*], and I had a splendid Christmas. She has to go back to Calgary after New Year's. We love each other, and we are planning on getting married after next harvest.

Before I went there for X-mas, I bought her a suitcase, a blanket for "Ma" and a box of cigars for "Pa." I arrived at the Petersens' at 10 a.m. Christmas morning and surprised them all. We had lunch at 12. At 4 o'clock we had a big turkey dinner with wine and whisky. We had a good time all evening. At 2 o'clock everybody else went to bed, while Emmie and I stayed up. We sat talking about our marriage for about an hour and a half. Then she went to bed with her mother and I with her father. The next day, her parents and her brother went to a funeral while I took her to the doctor at

Standard. I drove home at 5 p.m. On the way home, I stopped at Ray Schooling's and bought a radio.[48]

The Petersens

Emily Petersen, my mother, was living with her Danish-born parents on the family farm near Standard, along with her brothers, Herman, 22, and Walter, 17. Her sister, Vera Elliott, 26, and another brother, Sydney, 30, were both married and living nearby. Mother's parents, Mary and Jesse—also known as "J.J."—Petersen, had met and married in St. Paul, Minnesota, and had begun farming at Verdel, Nebraska, along with Grandmother's brother, Mike Christensen. As the family needed room to expand, Mike went searching, ending up at Standard in 1909, and it was he who wrote to the Petersens saying he had found "a paradise for the poor." In 1914 he built the Banner Hotel in Standard—still used today.

In 1910 the Petersens entrained to Gleichen, Alberta—first Grandfather, the boys, livestock, and household effects, later Grandmother and

The Petersen house and farm, c 1926.

---

48 Ray Schooling came to southern Alberta from Missouri in 1918. While working as a mechanic northeast of Standard, he bought land near Hussar where he and his bride, Agnes, farmed in 1921. Ray sold radios, charged up batteries, and, during the Depression, operated the Pacific grain elevator. Highly regarded, his electrical and mechanical skills made a major contribution to the community.

the younger children, following the prairie trail, by team and wagon, to Standard. This fledgling hamlet, founded on CPR land the year before, was quickly being settled by Danish immigrants from the United States and Denmark, becoming a very Danish settlement, (as was Dalum, further northeast), and Danish was heard everywhere in the community right through the 1930s.

Grandfather Petersen was an intelligent man, spoke six languages and had sailed many times around the world, but he knew little about farming. It was Grandmother, a hard-working, determined little woman, who ran the place, deciding what to seed and where and when it should be cut. By the late 1920s, their mixed farming operation, including large gardens, was well established. They had paid for their first farm. They were buying another, and a new car, and occasionally travelled to the States. Though father thought the Petersens were wealthy, when the Depression came, they were hit just as hard as everyone else. And they had had their share of illness. Mother would always remember the sound of her twenty-one-year-old brother, Alvin, screaming with pain during the summer of 1917, as he slowly succumbed to cancer.

Mother was twenty in 1928, 5′ 2″, blond-haired and blue-eyed. Because of hearing problems, she had dropped out of school at grade eight, and though she had wanted to study Interior Design in the States, her mother needed her at home. So farming was the only life mother knew, but she was a good cook, a hard worker and loved farm life. Her parents liked and respected father, and the feeling was mutual.

[*Diary*:] <u>December 29, 1928</u>. Got up at 8 o'clock. Hitched up four horses and had breakfast. Then took the horses and loaded a load of wheat onto Frank Thew's wagon. Halfway a tire blew on one wheel. Got a jack from Harper's truck and fixed it again. Arrived home at 5 o'clock. Loaded wheat for seed-wheat. Am waiting for Ray Schooling so he can put up my radio, but he keeps me waiting. On the way to "the chute," I saw Frank Draper.[49] He gave me a dog.

<u>December 30, 1928</u>. Got up at 9 o'clock. It snowed all day. No traces of Ray Schooling. Should go and see the girlfriend tomorrow. Have no way of getting there. Am supposed to play at a dance at Hussar tomorrow evening.

---

[49] Frank Draper was a bachelor who farmed ten or so miles west of father.

1929

Radios, with headsets, began appearing on the Prairies about 1926, and people out in the country were suddenly connected to the rest of the world. For father, it was deeply satisfying to hear music, both popular and classical—especially opera.

Radios in the 1920s were battery-powered by 1) rechargeable batteries—usually a car battery, which needed recharging about once a week—and 2) one or two higher voltage dry batteries, not rechargeable, but needing replacement about every third week. Depending on the amount of use, both types were a considerable expense. Also required was a high outside antenna, with wire about 100 feet long, insulators at each end, with a lead-in wire to the set, and a ground connection, i.e. a two or three foot iron pipe driven into the ground. Sound was provided by a loudspeaker, earphones, or both.[50]

Drought returned to most of southern Alberta in 1929, and crops were sparse.

Fri., January 4, 1929. Well! Now we have 1929. Yesterday Ray was here with the radio, and it is certainly fine. The music comes through fine. Yesterday I did not do much besides trying it out. Today I drove a load of wheat to Dorothy.

Sat., January 5, 1929. Today drove two loads of wheat to Dorothy (220 bushels). Today I drove all the way down to the elevator. For that I made $4.40.

Sun., January 6, 1929. Got up at 10:30 a.m. A little later, McKinney came, and we talked. Then I saw him home and rode over to Walt. He and I figured out that I had $162 owed to me. It was past midnight before I got home and did chores. Had Long Beach, California, on the radio (KFOX). Went to bed at 1:30.

Mon., January 7, 1929. Got up at 8 o'clock. Hauled a load of wheat (110 bushels) and loaded up another load. Chased some range horses out. Broke my axe down on the ice. Did the dishes (for the last two - three days). Went to bed at 11 o'clock.

Tues., January 8, 1929. Got up at 7 o'clock. Hauled two loads of wheat (220 bushels). At Dorothy I got an unexpected letter from Worley. He writes that he will pay me the 5 cents for hauling. And

---

[50] R. Grinder and G. Fathauer, *The Radio Collector's Directory and Price Guide*, (Scottsdale, Arizona: Ironwood Press, 1986), pp. 40-41; David and Betty Johnson, *Antique Radios* (Lombard, Illinois: Wallace-Homestead Book Company, 1985), pp. 8, 44.

also thinks we can agree on a price for the house. When I made supper, I found that most of the big salmon I had bought had gone bad. I boiled the best of it and gave the rest to the dog and the cats. It is the first time in a long time that the little kitten has stopped mewing.

It has become quite dangerous to go down the Dorothy hill these days, and if it does not improve soon, I think I shall haul to the "chute" again. Today I broke my rough-lock twice, and twice the one wheeler fell and was almost run over.[51] If Worley keeps his promise and pays 5 cents, I have made $11 today. It has snowed quite a bit lately, and today we had a chinook. Now, tonight, the wind is from the northwest and has turned cold, so perhaps we shall get a blizzard. Went to bed at 11 o'clock. It is a terrible life, this Bachelor Life.

Wed., January 9, 1929. Today hauled a load of wheat (120 bushels) and loaded another one. Was back home at 5:30. Stopped at Dorothy and had my dinner. Cleaned the barn after I got back. Had supper at 9 o'clock (fried fish & hot cakes). I'm just about all out of grub.

Thurs., January 10, 1929. Today hauled 223 bushels wheat. When I came home after the second load, I discovered about seventy head of range horses in my feed. Had to chase them out.

Fri., January 11, 1929. Stayed home today. Cleaned up in the house and cleaned out the barn. Fixed the corral fence. Went over to Schnapps and got my mail, had a letter from Emmie. She sent the negatives I've been asking for. Wrote a letter. Washed a bunch of towels.

Sat., January 12, 1929. Felt tough all day. Done nothing but chore around. Put up a fence across the lake to keep the range horses out.

Sun., January 13, 1929. Had a visit from Harold Thew. He stayed all night. We had a lot of good music on the radio.

Mon., January 14, 1929. Hauled 114 bushels. Harold is still with me. He had supper all ready when I got home. It sure was a treat. Had visit from Jimmy. He brought me a letter from Emmie; she's still in Calgary.

---

51 The rough-lock is a brake, preventing the wagon from running over the horses while going downhill. With more than two horses, those right in front of the wagon were called the "wheelers," being next to the wheels.

Dorothy, Feb. 4, 1929
Dear Gudrun and Alfred:

Perhaps it's time that I give you some signs of life from me, so I'll use the opportunity to send you a picture I took recently. It's not as good as it should be, I think I'm looking better than that, but it might give you an idea of me if nothing else. I have an odd look in one eye in the picture, but I think it's caused by the light.

We've had a severe winter this year—that's to say, after Christmas. Before Christmas it was the best winter Canada had had for years. But now it's the opposite. It's cold for certain. I haven't delivered all of my wheat yet. I stopped when it got so cold. I'll have lots of work next year, and I must do my own cooking, but I hope it will be my last year alone. Emily has been ill since December. She has an ear infection. Her parents have paid over $900 for her since December, and she's not well yet. But the doctor says that she'll recover in good condition.

How are things going at home? Do I still have some money in the bank at home? Maybe we'll come home next winter, and it would help things considerably if I had some money to help out.

I'm extremely well, and don't know what else I can say. I'm ending with love to everyone, big and small from yours,

Sincerely, Helge

[*Diary*:] Tues., February 12, 1929. On January 20, I moved over to Earl Bryant's, my neighbour, because it got too cold in the shack on Stony Ridge. I still have about 1,000 bushels to haul. The thermometer has reached 50 below, and it has been icy cold for a long while. I am still at Earl's. The last couple of days, it warmed up again, so today we tried to get some wheat I had lying on the ground. There was a lot of snow in it, and we could not get the snow out, so we drove over to Ross's, and I sold it for hog feed for 55 cents a bushel. I believe there are about forty bushels. Today is the day Emmie is in Calgary to get the last operation over and done with. I hope it will not be too hard for her. On Sunday, February 3, I went to visit her. I rode over there on my saddle horse. It is not too far if I go across the country. It was mostly because I felt so bad about being so far away from her next summer, and I have been thinking of giving up this place and working for her father and then maybe get a farm over there next year. But lately I have started changing my mind again, and I have written a long letter to Worley.

Fri., February 15, 1929. Yesterday night I was at a dance down at Dorothy. Chester Thew and I played with Mr. Kidd.[52] The grocer at Dorothy "chorded" us on the piano. There was quite a good turnout and everybody had a good time. I was taken outside several times for a toast. I had gin and Concord wine. We played until 4 o'clock in the morning and made $6 apiece. I have not heard from Emmie since the operation, but Mrs. Thew was in Calgary and said that she saw Emmie at the Hotel Empress. So at least I know she is alive.

Sun., February 17, 1929. McKinney and Abe were over here at Earl's, together with Harold Thew and stayed here for dinner. After dinner I won a pair of chaps from Abe by flipping a coin with him. Today I caught Fanny, so now I have all four horses in Earl's barn. Today I gave McKinney $10 for payment for part of what I owe him.

Tues., February 19, 1929. This morning we had a terrible blizzard. This afternoon it stopped, and I drove over to Dutch Bryant's and borrowed a sleigh and then drove over to Stony Ridge and loaded a grain tank on it. Yesterday Earl and I moved two of my granaries. After that I rode down to Dorothy and got two letters, one from Emmie dated February 8th. She wrote that she would not promise to stay home from dances this summer and did not think that it was worth it for me to toil all summer to make enough money for a home for her, because she did not know yet what she wanted to do next winter. Well, that was not such an encouraging letter. She also writes that Vera [*Elliott, her sister*] is still at home.[53]

I had a letter from Harper. He writes that he will need cash for his horses. Last night I had a new idea. I am thinking of getting a job at the Pool Elevator. I will have to work as a helper the first year, and maybe I will get an elevator the following year. I can farm Stony Ridge this summer anyway. I will see if I can get in touch with Ralph Armstrong [*Alberta Wheat Pool agent, Hussar*] first chance I get. The other day, I sent my radio battery to town to get it charged. Yesterday Thews brought it out again. But McKinney took it home and put it in his radio, so now I will take his instead. I have still not heard from Emmie since her operation. I tried to

---

[52] Russell Kidd, age twenty-six, built a grocery store at Dorothy in 1928, as the railroad track was being laid. A gregarious, popular man, and a jokester, Kidd ran the store for three years, enjoyed his customers and liked to party.

[53] This meant that my parents had a chance of running the second Petersen farm which Vera and her husband had been leasing.

phone Standard while I was at Dutch's, but their telephone at Standard was "out of order."

Thurs., February 21, 1929. Today Earl Bryant and I hauled 160 bushels to the "chute"; we will continue until we have finished. Today I had a letter from Worley with a cheque for $135. I also had a letter from Emmie. She wrote it in Calgary. She suffers terribly from the operations in her nose. She has to go back to Calgary for two - three weeks after she has come home again. I will go to Calgary with her the next time. She wrote a happier letter this time. In her last letter, she did not mean that she would go to dances with other men, but that she would go with her family when they went and I could not take her. She thinks that she would suffer living here at Stony Ridge, and she thinks that we could raise sheep.

Vera Elliott, Emily's sister, with her horse, Ace. Standard, 1929.—Courtesy, Earl Elliott

Sat., February 23, 1929. Earl and I are still hauling wheat. Today we hauled 220 bushels.When we came home, I had to start the pump-engine [*to water stock*], and when it started, the crank flew up and hit my lower lip, and I got a bump on my lip.

Sun., February 24, 1929. Again today Earl and I hauled 220 bushels. We have chinook weather these days. And I shall just make it the last minute if this weather holds up. We reckon it will take us two days more before we have finished. McKinney was over here and brought my battery; he has used it for three days.

Wed., February 27, 1929. Yesterday we finished with the wheat. Today I took Pete & Topsy and borrowed Frank Draper's cutter and drove to Hussar. Chester Thew drove with me. In Hussar I went around and paid all my bills, and then I met Joe Aasris. He is trying to start up a new orchestra. We agreed to meet for practice next Wednesday. At around 3 o'clock, I drove to the Petersens' in

Chancellor. When I got there, "Father-in-law" told me that Emmie was seriously ill and was in the hospital. And I thought she was well and at home. That was quite a disappointment, but "Dad" said that he and Herman meant to go to Calgary tomorrow, so I will go with them.

Thurs., February 28, 1929. Today we went to Calgary in Petersens' Studebaker. When we reached the Hotel Empress, they told us at the office that Emmie and her mother were up in number 39, so we went up. I will say that Emmie was happily surprised. She had come back from the hospital yesterday and looked like a corpse. It turned out that after the last operation she had had a relapse. And had the most terrible pains in her ears, and finally she could not stand the pains any longer, and Doc sent her to the hospital where she could get opium, etc. Here she was for a couple of days, but the nurses did not take good care of her, and she had a nose bleed and bled for half an hour before the nurse came, and after that it took them two hours to get it stopped. So Doc sent her back to the hotel. She can hardly hear. I stayed at the hotel all day and kept Emmie company. She is up and around, but that is all.

Sat., March 2, 1929. Am still in Calgary. Emmie's parents went home today, but I shall stay until Monday so she will not be too lonesome. She will be completely cured, and Doc thinks that she can go home next Friday. We went up to the Strand today and took in a movie. Mon., March 4, 1929. Went to Standard by train. Emmie went to the station to say good-bye. She looks better now than when I saw her last Thursday. At Standard I met Walter and Herman, and they took me back to Petersens' in Walt's coupe.

Tues., March 5, 1929. Had thought of going home today. But a strong wind blew, so instead I stayed and helped Herman clean the barn.

Emily's brothers, Herman and Walter Petersen, c 1926.

Wed., March 6, 1929. Drove to Hussar today. The snow has all gone, and I had a difficult trip. At Hussar I put the horses up in a stable and counted on having an orchestra practice, but it turned out that they had practised Monday instead. However, Manville, Mrs. Smith and I had a good practice at Andersons anyway, and I stayed at Hussar overnight. Saw Steve Hale, and he will sell me his coupe for $160, $50 down and $15 a month.
Thurs., March 7, 1929. Drove home today. I got as far as Carter's place when my cutter broke down, and I had a bad time with it. I got an old fence post at Carter's and put it on for a runner. But the cutter is ruined, and I will have to buy Frank Draper a new one ($15). I slept at Earl Bryant's.
Fri., March 8, 1929. Today I moved over to my shack again. I also went down to Dorothy for a registered letter [*enclosing an inheritance cheque*] which was supposed to wait for me there, but Kidd could not find it.
Sat., March 9, 1929. Went to Dorothy again today. I started the old Ford and drove down in that. Kidd says that he has lost my letter. He believes it must have gone with some letters he mailed at Drumheller.
Sun., March 10, 1929. Drove over to the Bryants' and brought Mrs. Bryant over to the Thews' where Chester and I practised. I was also over at Schang's to see when he can come to fix my barn, etc.
Mon., March 11, 1929. First drove over to Schang's and tried to get Walt to solder a radiator for me, but he was busy fixing McKinney's Chevrolet. So I tried to solder it myself but had no success, so I drove over to the Thews. When I got there, Chester was ready, and we drove to Hussar. Here I saw Steve Hale, and he sold me a Ford coupe for $170, $50 cash and $15 a month. We practised with the orchestra and slept at the Chinese's.
Tues., March 12, 1929. Chester took the old Ford home for me, and I drove the coupe over to the Petersens'. Emmie came home yesterday and looked quite pretty. I took her for a car-ride, and we stayed up until 1:30.
Wed., March 13, 1929. Today everybody drove to Vera's farm, and Emmie and I were home alone. The others came home at 5 o'clock, and I had supper and drove over to Hussar. I shall go with Emmie to Calgary on the 25th of this month. At Hussar I practised with the orchestra and drove home at 11 o'clock. Was at home about 2 a.m.
Thurs., March 14, 1929. Cleaned my barn and all over the place. Washed the car.

Fri., March 15, 1929. Drove over to Schang's and tried to get him to finish my barn. He would not promise to come until next Wednesday. He is not going to farm that place this year, so he sold me his drill for $140 including six "horse eveners." I also bought three geese from him. From there I drove to Hussar. Here I telephoned the Petersens and told them that Harper's sale would be on the 23rd of this month. I tried to speak to Emmie, but she was too deaf to hear me. Vera told that they would be coming to Hussar for the amateur performance. That started at 8 o'clock. We (the orchestra) opened with "You Tell Me Your Dreams," and between 1st and 2nd act Mrs. Smith and I played "Hungarian Dance" and [*"Kuyawiak"?*]. Sure enough, after the performance I found Walt, Herman and Vera. We played dance music then, and I had a dance with Vera. After it was over, I drove home and slept until 11 o'clock the next day.

Sat., March 16, 1929. Drove over to Earl Bryant's with some cups I had bought for him yesterday. Took Earl with me over to Currie. Asked Currie if I could use his fanning mill.[54] After that we drove over to Schang's, and I settled with him. Had supper at Earl Bryant's.

Sun., March 17, 1929. Slept in this morning. Before I had breakfast I went out to catch the horses. Had quite a bit of trouble with them, and at last I had to start the car and chase them with it. After breakfast I took four horses and went over to Schang's. I got the sowing machine and also bought four sections of harrows and one set of harness, so now we are square.

Mon., March 18, 1929. Drove over to Earl Bryant's and took a team of his horses together with Pete & Topsy and hauled a load of wheat home for him. We fanned wheat until late into the evening, and because we did not finish, I stayed all night.

Tues., March 19, 1929. Finished fanning Earl's wheat. And Lyle & Earl came over and started their John Deere tractor up and pulled my last granary home beside the barn. Meanwhile, I moved the fanning mill over, and we were all set by noon. I made dinner, and we cleaned 200 bushels after dinner. Lyle & Earl stayed here over night so we can finish early tomorrow.

---

54 Fanning mills separated grain from weed seeds, dust and chaff, through the use of forced air. Grading the grain were various sizes of screens, kept from clogging by moving brushes. The best grade of grain, being heavier, fell below. Generally powered by small gas engines, some models were turned by hand or electricity.

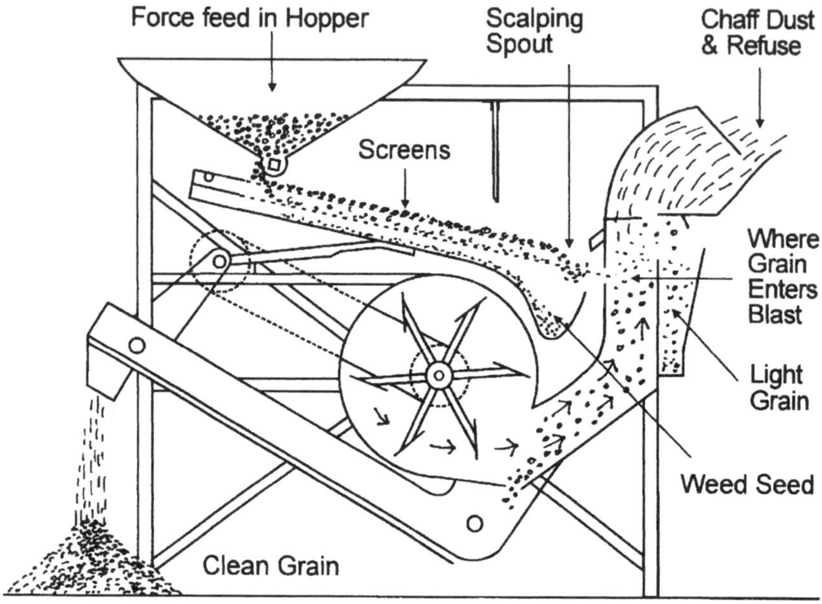

A Fanning mill—the Aero Grain and Seed Cleaner, built by AGR Link Manufacturing Co., Portage La Prairie, Manitoba, 1928. —Courtesy, GAA

Wed., March 20, 1929. Today finished cleaning my wheat, and I found out that I was fifty bushels short. Lyle took the mill over to Bush's farm which they have rented this year. I moved their harrow and disc over from Harper's place.

Sat., March 23, 1929. I went to Harper's sale and bought three horses, one wagon & hay rack, four horse collars, etc., value $170.

Sun., March 31, 1929. I am back again after having been away all week, and many things have happened during that week. Last Sunday I drove to Chancellor where I found Emmie doing well after her illness. We had a nice evening. Monday everybody else went to a sale while Emmie and I stayed at home. Tuesday I drove Emmie and her parents to Calgary. We arrived at 2 p.m. We went up to Dr. Spankie. And went to a show in the evening. Wednesday was spent seeing the doctor, etc.

Later I found out that there was a big prairie fire out around my farm. But more about that later. Thursday at 12 o'clock, I took Emmie to General Hospital where she had an operation on her nose. At 3:30 her father, mother and I drove over to visit her. She told us she had had some terrible pains. Later in the evening, I went to see her again. Friday at 12 o'clock, I took Emmie back to the hotel again. We stayed in there until Saturday; Emmie will have to stay there for some time yet. Saturday I drove her parents to their home, and I stayed there until Sunday. When I was leaving, Mrs. Petersen gave me six hens and a rooster to take home. When I came home, I found Currie at the house and two of his horses in the stable. He told me then about the great prairie fire. It had started Tuesday in the great hurricane wind which sparked an old burnt down straw stack to new life, and the sparks flew out into the grass, and in a short while the fire had spread all over. My farm would have burned down if Earl Bryant and Currie had not come over here and fought it with wet blankets. The Bunney farm had burnt down completely, and Currie's & Whitney's barn & granaries [*filled with grain*] burned down.[55] The fire went all the way to Saskatchewan. Today got my Ford license, letters from Alfred and Maren Johanne, the Wheat Pool, etc.

Hussar, Alta., April 3, 1929
Dear Gudrun & Alfred!

Thank you for the letter which I received a couple of days ago. You had no need to apologize for tardiness in answering my letter; it's a constant weakness of mine!

It just happens that I have a good chance to reply today. It was intended that we should start the fieldwork today, but it started to blow something awful overnight, and today we are having a real old fashioned blizzard. The snow is whirling so hard that you cannot see ten feet in front of you. That's how it goes in this country. Yesterday it was almost summer, and we were already to go. The horses have been in the barn getting grain fed, so they can stand the hard work in the field—and today it is winter again. It is not that the snow is not welcome. The ground is awful dry. Up until January 15th, the weather was warm, almost like fall, but then it got cold with vengeance—we had, during three weeks, an average temperature of 40 below with strong winds, but no snow. In March

---

[55] The Bunneys were away at the time of the fire, returning to find their ranch in ruins—all their buildings, most of the grass and hay, as well as some stock in the barn, were gone. The fire had reached such proportions that neighbours had been unable to save the animals. The Bunneys gave up ranching, sold their property, and moved to BC, where they operated a hay farm. (Roen, *Dorothy*, p. 119). The Whitneys, also among the earliest settlers, are now gone. The Elmer Currie family, having emigrated from Washington State two years before, were left with only a tarpaper shack, an outhouse, the singed horses, and the two milk cows Elmer had driven into a slough area. The Curries persevered, however, and descendants live in the area today.

it warmed up again with sunshine and dry weather. Two weeks ago, we experienced the worst prairie fire this country has seen for many years. Alfred! If you should wish to see something thrilling but awful, a prairie fire will do it. All it takes to start it is a careless cigarette dropped in the grass! The day it happened I was in Calgary with my girl friend, while she was getting her nose operated on, but more about that later.

A terrific wind came up suddenly, and around dinnertime neighbours discovered a cloud of smoke in the distance. They jumped in their cars, taking along wet gunnysacks and forks. They found that the fire had started about a mile from my place (south), and the wind was blowing from the northwest. The fires travelled faster than a horse could run. It is impossible to stop such a fire by trying to put it out. The only thing that can be done is to start a "back-fire," which means that you start a small fire a long distance away and try to make it run against the wind. That is how they managed to stop that fire a quarter of a mile from my house. The fire burnt a strip of land twenty miles wide by forty miles long. A neighbour of mine was burnt out completely—buildings, feed and grain—all went. Another neighbour had most of his horses burnt by the fire, backing them into a corner, where they could not get away on account of the barbed wire. I have a few of them that survived the ordeal in my barn now, doctoring them the best I can. If the neighbours had not discovered the fire when they did, I would not have had a thing left! In Denmark such a thing would not be possible, but it can get awful dry here on the prairie.

I see by your letter, that you are under the impression that I own 10 horses, but I have only 8 at the present. When I wrote my last letter, I had intended to buy 6 horses, but I changed my mind. I have since bought 4 others. I have rented a section of land, half a mile wide and two miles long. A section contains 640 acres, but the land is not all under cultivation. I have 280 acres ready for crop this year, and I intend to break up 100 acres of new land. When I'm seeding I'll be using 6 horses on the seed drill, and I will be able to seed 20 - 25 acres a day. When I start plowing, I will use 6 horses for the plow; I can plow about three acres a day.

When harvest comes, I use 4 horses for the binder, and can cut fifteen acres a day. Then I haul the threshed grain to the railroad. Then I turn the horses loose, and they can rustle for themselves most of the winter. If bad weather comes, they can find shelter and feed at the straw stacks left by the threshing machines. These horses are not anything like the Danish horses, which would be done for the very first blizzard they had to face. The farm I have rented belongs to a dentist in Spokane, USA. He supplies half the seed and pays for half the cost of threshing for half the crop. Thus, if it is a good year, he will make more money than in a poor year. It is very hard for me to tell you what my net income amounts to, as most of my earnings go to buying horses or machinery.

As yet I don't know what I will get for my wheat. I am a member of the Alberta Wheat Pool and will get paid in four installments. However, I'm expecting a gross income of $1,600, with a possible net income of $600. I will not be able to afford a trip to Denmark next year; still, if I don't go pretty soon, it may never be. You will realize how far a man can travel when he has a wife and children. But I understand by Alfred's letter that it is the only way I can get the money waiting for me in Denmark.[56] I am also quite anxious to get father's violin, and I have so many fond memories of Denmark. Emily is strong enough to stand up to the life of a farm wife. She was born and raised on the farm and has lived there all her life. I told you that she speaks Danish, but she speaks with the dialect of the southern Jutland people, and she gets embarrassed when I speak my city dialect. But surely we will be able to get along somehow. This fall she was taken with a sickness that still has a hold of her. She developed a growth in her nose, and it has worked up into her ear, with matter running from both nose and ear. Her eardrums are so swollen that she is quite deaf. She goes to a specialist in Calgary, who claims he can cure her, but it will take some time. It is very painful. However, she does not want me to know about the pain. She is twenty-one years of age, and I'm sending you a couple of pictures of her. They are not the best of her. Those I'm keeping for myself until such time when I have her for myself.

Her parents are very nice people, and I have found a new home there. I sincerely hope she will recover. She is not very enthusiastic about me taking off for Denmark, though she thinks I should go before we get married. But if she won't travel, I won't either, as we can use all the money we can get a hold of.

I earned about $41 with my violin last year. If I only lived a little closer to Hussar, I could get a lot of violin pupils, but maybe

---

[56] This is the money sent in the lost registered letter, the inheritance from father's Aunt Larsen, in Denmark.

I'm just as well off without them. How much in Canadian funds is 1490 kr? [*in July 1929, $406*]. It is so seldom that I see the exchange rates in the papers. I'm so thankful to Alfred for looking after my money in Denmark! I often wonder about my prospects should I go back to Denmark; somehow, they don't look very bright to me? At the same time, I like it over here, and I sincerely wish that you folks in Denmark could come over and visit me. I might as well wish you could travel to the moon. Meanwhile, I cannot promise anything until harvest time.

Please convey my greetings to all—and Vilhelm, Else and the children,

Love from Helge

[*Diary*:] Tues., April 16, 1929. During the first part of March, I was up in Calgary with Emmie again. She was in the hospital again. When I came home again, I started getting ready seeding. On Saturday the 13th, I seeded about ten acres, but then we had a snowstorm. Then on Monday, I phoned the Petersens and asked if Emmie had come home, and when they said yes, I drove up there.

The ears of Ole's horses are cocked toward him, as he proudly photographed his team while seeding, 1928 or 1929.

Sat., June 22, 1929. Well! Now I had forgotten the diary again. I have 180 acres with wheat and need some rain badly. Today I left home after dinner and drove up to Emmie. An awfully dry wind blew. And just before I reached Chancellor, I noticed that the engine started hammering. I stopped and checked the oil, and it was all right, so I drove on. I arrived at the Petersens' at supper time. After supper I drove Emmie to Standard. The engine continued hammering, so when we got to Standard, I drove the car to the garage and asked them to tighten the con-rods while we went to the cinema. When we came out, they told me at the garage that the oil pump of the engine was plugged so we got Sydney Busch [*Emily's brother-in-law*] to take us home. I can't get the car until Monday noon.

Sun., June 23, 1929. Tried hard all morning to get the folks to come out to see my place today; and I sure had a hard time as Mama was sore because I was supposed to have come last Sunday and didn't come because it was raining. Finally, around dinner, I got them persuaded, and we left about 1 o'clock—"Pa," "Mama," Emmie and I. I had made arrangements with Mrs. Bryant to cook a little lunch for us, so we went by Earl's place and took the lunch with us. The folks seemed to like the place all right and said that the crop looked all right. We had the lunch and drove down to look at Dorothy hill [*possibly where the new road was being built*] and got home to Petersens' place at 8 o'clock.

Emily's parents, Mary and Jesse Petersen, finally agreed to visit Ole's place at Stony Ridge. Emily in doorway, June 23, 1929.

Mon., June 24, 1929. This morning I took the folks out to Vera's place. She has a nice place and a nice little three-roomed house. But the roads out there are a fright (rough). We had dinner at Vera's place and went home right after, about 4 o'clock. "Pa" took me to Standard, where they had my car ready, and I drove it home again, and was figuring on keeping on going east. But my eyelids started to get sore yesterday, and at last I decided to stay and go with the folks to Calgary tomorrow.

Tues., June 25, 1929. Left Petersens' at 9:30 and got to Calgary 11:40. Emmie went right to the Doc. And I went to the optician about my glasses which were broken. We ran around town all day shopping. I saw Doc Spankie and got some dope to put in my eyes. At night we went to a show in the Strand and left Calgary at 11 o'clock. Got to Petersens' at 1:20—(muddy roads in places). I changed over to my car and reached Stony Ridge at 5 o'clock.
Wed., June 26, 1929. About 9 o'clock McKinney woke me up and talked to me—he wanted my horses for a week plowing. Got up a little lost. Went over to Earl Bryant's with some groceries. While there we had a dandy rain that'll keep the wheat going another week.
Thurs., June 27, 1929. Caught Pete & Topsy this morning and hauled the posts & wire out for the last mile of fence. In the afternoon, I went over to Thews' to practise for the show coming Saturday. Stayed with Mrs. Smith for supper.
Fri., June 28, 1929. Left after dinner. Went to Hussar. Practised with Manville and got to Petersens' before supper. After supper Emmie & I went to Hussar. The dance went over big. We sure had a swell lunch made especially for the orchestra. Emmie enjoyed it fine! Got back to Petersens' at 4 o'clock. Went to bed in guest room.
Sat,. June 29, 1929. Got up at 6 o'clock. Helped the folks with the chores. Slept in bunkhouse from 9 - 12. In afternoon Emily & I went for a walk to look at the crop. Awful dry. Left at 7 o'clock. Played for picture show. Got home at 1 o'clock.
Sun., June 30, 1929. Got up at 10 o'clock. After breakfast heard some cars—it was a bunch going to picnic. Joined them. Had a good time. Played baseball.
Mon., July 1, 1929. Wrote a letter to Emmie. Earl Bryant stopped here on his way to Ross's. Had a talk with him. Went out to look at wheat. Turning yellow. Awful dry. Crop looks sick.
Tues., July 2, 1929. While I was out fencing, saw two fellows walking across the field. They stopped at my shack as I came in to see who it was—Roy Robinson & his man.[57] They were walking home, having broken their plow while working on Doc Thompson's half section west. After dinner Jack Zorky came, and he & I went for a swim. While I was fencing in the afternoon, a car came along, and behold, it was Herman, Vera & Bill. They were out looking for

[57] The Robinsons, among the earliest families in the district, lived immediately west of the Bunneys.

poles. So I jumped in my car, and we went south two miles where George Frownfelter was fencing. Found out where CPR quarter was in coulee. And went by Earl Bryant's on way home, where I got a can of water. Herman went ahead. When I got home, hurried up to clean out the shack a bit first. Saw some women's clothes lying on the bed but thought Herman had played a joke on me. Got shack swept out and went down after the folks. Found out that there were three girls out swimming and a man dressing in the workshop. Found out it was McKinney & the Bush girls. Showed the folks the shack. And went with them down to George's coulee. Showed the place to cut poles and left them at George's west gate. An awful strong hot wind blowing today.
Wed., July 3, 1929. Was fencing. The wheat is drying out fast. Can't stand another week without rain. It's heading out.
Thurs., July 4, 1929. Earl Bryant borrowed my car to go to town in. Had a dandy big shower in afternoon. Was fencing.
Sat., July 6, 1929. Went to Hussar. Got a registered letter from Alfred with $406 [*inheritance from his Aunt Larsen in Denmark*]. Also cheque from Worley, $65. Paid Life Insurance Co. $121, Hoiland $91, Pacific Finance $15.[58] Sent $18 to Eatons. Went on to Petersens' to take Emmie to dance, but she couldn't go, had a severe cold. Walter went along instead. Got back to McKinney's at 9 o'clock as it started to sprinkle. Didn't expect a crowd, as it looked bad. But crowd came soon. And they danced until 4 o'clock while it was steadily pouring down outside. Chester and Manville & I played. Had to put chains on tires in McKinney's barn. Drove home where Walt & I slept until noon.

Hussar, Alta., July 6, 1929
Dear Gudrun & Alfred!

Thank you so very much for the letter and money which I received today. It was really wonderful of you to act so quickly, and I must confess that they arrived at a very convenient time. My life insurance policy is due, in fact it should have been paid a couple of weeks ago, but I will be able to make out now. We have had a very peculiar summer this year as far as the crop goes.

The first part of the summer was terribly dry, and it is only a week ago that the bubble burst (I mean rain), and now we get a good shower every now and again, and it looks like we may get a

---

[58] Ed Hoiland had a John Deere Agency, service shop and garage in Hussar.

pretty good crop. However, there are thousands of farmers here in Alberta who are completely out-of-luck for this year—the rain came too late! My wheat is awful short, but it seems to be pretty well filled out. We could have prospects for a good price this fall.

Emily is in fair health these days. Gudrun was asking just what is the matter with her? It is a long story, but as far as I can understand from the doctor, a few years ago, she developed a growth in her nose. It kept growing towards her ear, and finally became so painful that she had to go to the doctor. But, in the meantime, it caused an awful lot of infection, and the matter kept building up pressure until she could not stand it any longer. It is a very serious disease, and hard to cure. Several times during the winter, the doctor operated on the infected area, so that it would be contained in her face and not cause germs to spread. He said that he had got the worst of it but that it would be next summer before she was completely cured. And once completely cured, it would never come back again. During this summer, she has gone to Calgary regularly once a week.

I have been busy fencing around my fields and helping to make a [*graded*] road to Dorothy where we will haul our grain this fall.

I'm still in my usual good health, and send you all my love.

Helge

[*Diary*:] Sun., July 7, 1929. Drove up to Petersens'. Bad roads. Got there at suppertime.

Mon., July 8, 1929. Left Petersens' with Emmie & MacMaster [*a friend of Emily's*] at 7 o'clock. Drove to Standard. Took taxi to Calgary. Got there in time to see big Stampede parade. After parade went with Emily to Doctor. Bad cold! Had to have dose of voxine made. At night went to Stampede ground, saw big exhibition of machinery & cars. Went to vaudeville until 10 o'clock. Took a taxi to Empress Hotel. Took Emily to a room and slept on a cot in Mac's room at "Empress."

Tues., July 9, 1929. Went shopping in the morning and to the fair grounds in afternoon.

Left Calgary at 11 o'clock p.m. in taxi. Went to Petersens' in the old Ford where I left Emily and drove on home. Got home 6 a.m.

Wed., July 10, 1929. Slept until 12 noon.

Thurs., July 11, 1929. Went over to McKinney to borrow his double disc and wound up buying it for $50, paid him half cash; paid him also for the rest of wheat hauled.

Fri., July 12, 1929. Was discing. Had six horses. Had them hooked 3 + 3 in the forenoon but decided to change them to six abreast after dinner. They've started to grade the road from my NW corner to Dorothy.

Sat., July 13, 1929. Was supposed to work on the road, but when I got there, there was nobody in sight, so I went home by Earl Bryant's. Took Earl & Barbara to town, where we got groceries. Phoned Emmie. Bought Earl's sulky plow for $25.

Wed., July 17, 1929. This week I've been discing. Today I was working on the road, driving fresno [*an earth-moving scoop*]. Harold Thew told me he was going to take Mary Law to dance in Chancellor, so I asked him to phone Emmie and ask her to go with me.[59] We've had some awful hot winds and no rain, and the crop is drying out fast. I don't know how I can harvest it, as it is so short.

Fri., November 16, 1929. It was not a very big harvest I had this year. I have bought myself a new Ford "roadster" (that is to say paid $400 down for it). All my money has been spent. I have broken off with Emily Petersen as it looks hopeless with her ear. I play for a lot of dances. Have just written letters to Denmark, to Alfred and Vilhelm. Tonight I am going to play at a dance up at Bryant schoolhouse.

Ole with his new, briefly owned, Model A Ford Roadster, 1929.

Tues., November 19, 1929. Washed clothes all day. After supper I went over and picked up Earl Bryant, and together we went to a Wheat Pool meeting which was held at Duck Lake schoolhouse. Mr. Pettinger was the speaker.

[59] Mary Law had moved west with her parents from Manitoba to Chancellor, where she received her schooling. While taking nurses' training at Calgary, she met Harold Thew at a dance where his brother Chester (Dutch) played. She and Harold would marry in 1932, eventually buying the Harper place.

Cliff Burns bought Roany's colt from me for $10. Was home again at 10:30.

Thurs., December 5, 1929. Have moved over to Harold Thew's. There are three of us (Harold, Ralph Johnson & me).

Fri., December 6, 1929. Played at a dance at Dorothy. This afternoon I first phoned Louis Hoeght [*who played banjo*], and he said he could not find a car to drive out here in, so I had to go to Hussar to get him. Then we drove to Dorothy at 8:30 and were there shortly after 9 o'clock. It was a very poor gathering. There were about twenty-five men and six ladies. So it was a poor dance, and we stopped at 2:15. On the way home, we (Ralph and I) drove up to the Duck Lake farm where there also was a dance. Here it was still going full blast. So I danced a few dances, but they had a poor orchestra. So they all begged me to take out the violin, and at last I gave in. And then it went full blast until 6 o'clock in the morning. Then we drove home. Louis Hoeght returned to Hussar with somebody from there. When we came home, we found Ed and Harold. They had just returned from Standard. Then we made breakfast and fed the cattle.

Sat., December 7, 1929. Did the dishes and went to bed at 9 in the morning. At 1 p.m. I got up and drove over to Sieu Lake school where there was a Pool meeting. We started a "Pool local," and I was elected secretary and treasurer. Drove home at 5 o'clock. Lay down and rested for about an hour. Changed, and at 8 o'clock we drove over to Wintering Hills school. Ralph [*Johnson*] was with me. We had a sip of whisky before we left home, so we would not fall asleep on the road. We made it there at 9:30. Played there all night, and it was an excellent dance. It was a "shadow social" which means that just before supper a blanket was hung over a corner of the hall and a light was placed in the background of the corner. Then each lady had to stand in front of the light so you could see her shadow, but nothing else, and the gentlemen then bid on them. The highest bidder for each shadow took her to supper. Most of them went for about $2. I got Lulu Armstrong for $1.75. We stopped at 3:30. In the meantime, Ralph had taken my car to pick up the teacher from the Two-Bar School, but went into a snowdrift and was stuck. So, after the dance, I had to trudge for a couple of miles where we struggled until we got it out. Went to bed at 6 o'clock in the morning. Phew, was I ever tired.

Fri., December 13, 1929. Played at a dance at Two-Bar. There was too much snow to take the car, so I wrapped the violin and rode over to Fred Buck's on a saddle horse (nine miles). I was just in time for supper. The Bucks were also going to the dance, so I drove with them to the school in a cutter. The dance was poor; it was 30 degrees below zero F. and not a very large crowd. Besides, I was alone; Louis could not get out. We stopped at 3 o'clock. I was back here at 6:30 a.m.

Sat., December 14, 1929. Played for a dance at Atlas [*seven miles north of Hussar*]. We were able to get there by car, but it was a tough trip; it took us four hours to drive about twenty-two miles. Louis came out with Jerry Keener. There was a good crowd, and everybody had a good time. Just before supper, the teacher went around and stuck a little bow on all the ladies. After that all the men each got an envelope with a bow in. All the ladies' bows were different, and each gentleman then had to go around and find the matching bow. After that he took the lady concerned over to a set of scales, weighed her and had to pay 1 cent a pound after which he had supper with her. I was lucky and got one of Clarence Harmer's girls; she weighed 45 lbs[*?*].[60] We stopped at 4 o'clock. Were home at 7 o'clock in the morning. Was dead tired.

Thurs., December 25, 1929. Today drove over to the Nat Bryants' and had a delicious roast turkey. Played cards in the evening. I switched Nat's radio batteries around; he was too afraid to do it himself.

Mon., December 30, 1929. Drove to Hussar in the car. When I found out that the road to Calgary was passable, I decided to go to Calgary. Mrs. [*Loretta*] Donovan and Bembell were at Hussar where they were waiting for the train to Calgary. So they went with me to Calgary. We made it in 2½ hours. Saw a few picture shows.

Tues., December 31, 1929. Today went up to the Wheat Pool offices and found there Mr. Purdy, "general manager." We had a good talk about Pool locals, and I told him that in time I should like to become a Pool agent. He introduced me to Mr. McCloud, superintendent of the elevators. I also got quite a bit of literature about the Pool and an application form which I shall send in June.

---

60 Clarence Harmer and his father arrived on the prairies from Oregon in 1910, before there was a Hussar or a nearby railway. Leaving their horses and effects at Bassano, they looked for work at the Lawson and Treend ranches and ended up haying for the CPR. Clarence did very well in his ventures, finally buying land north of Hussar. He married Louise McInenly who had a son and three daughters. They then had two daughters of their own—one of whom possibly brought father's lunch.

Ran a few other errands and went to the Capitol at 11 p.m. where I saw a show called "Flight." That sure was a good movie. We went out at 1:30, and what a row in the streets. The [*New Year's*] rioters had pushed cars out in the middle of the streets, so traffic was blocked and the police were powerless. Went to bed at 3:30.

"Till the Good Times Come Again" 1930-1939

1930

Emily Petersen and Ole Nissen, prior to their break-up in 1929.

Headlines in The Calgary Herald read: "Great Din Meets New Year As It Reaches Calgary," "Traffic Blocked And Tangled On 8th Avenue," "A City Shouted Joy." The paper exclaimed: "Capacity audiences saw midnight previews at the Capitol and Palace theatres. New Year's greetings were flashed on the screen at midnight. A New Year with great things in store, had been ushered in. "

But the new year did not have great things in store. Following the stock market crash in 1929, the Great Depression began. The drought was already so severe that the Petersens would begin losing horses to sand colic, wherein the horses would pull up the scarce, short grass—roots and all—causing several pounds of dirt to settle in their stomachs. Before long they would quit eating. Nothing could be done about it.

For father, the Great Depression hit suddenly and forcefully.

[*Diary*:] Wed., January 1, 1930. Got up at 9 o'clock and saw that it had started blowing and snowing. That scared me, so I drove home. The Donovans came with me again.

Fri., January 10, 1930. Played at a dance at Dorothy. Ed went to Hussar to pick up Louis Hoeght. McKinney drove with us down there. We had a couple of McKinney's saddle horses for my sleigh, and we were like sardines in a tin. I had Lola on my lap, but had to lift her up once in a while as my leg fell asleep. We left for home at 3 o'clock and were home at 5:30. Slept until 1 p.m.

Dorothy, Alta., March 14, 1930

Dear Gudrun & Alfred!

As usual I'm late in answering your letter. One reason is that we are having very hard times here, and I don't want to answer your letter until I have made you acquainted with the situation over here. The fact is that never has the USA or Canadian farmer been in so desperate a financial situation. Food is just as bad; I imagine that the newspapers in Denmark must be full of the bad news. I will try to explain the circumstances the best I can. Last year both Canada and Argentina had very poor crops, so, of course, we expected a good price for our wheat this year, as we certainly didn't get a bumper crop.

Nevertheless, Canada is now sitting with 300 million bushels of wheat that nobody wants to buy. The price of wheat was $1.25 last fall; we expected it to go up to at least $1.75. So the farmers borrowed money on their wheat instead of selling it. Then the price started to go down day after day. I said borrowed, but they actually only took an advance on later deliveries. The price kept on sliding down, until the farmer was forced to sell the wheat. However, some of them did not deliver their wheat, thinking that the price was bound to go up again. Today the price is 78 cents, and thousands of farmers had to guarantee delivery of their wheat in order to hang on to their commitments, even selling their seed wheat to do so. Fifty-five percent of the Alberta farmers (I'm one of them) are members of Alberta Wheat Pool, and we have received 82 cents a bushel for the wheat we have delivered. We expect three more payments once our wheat is delivered. [*When father translated this letter in 1973, he added:* We never got a red cent more, as it turned out that we had already been overpaid].

The whole trouble lies with the "Wheat Kings" [*Grain Exchange*]; they are fighting the Wheat Pool, trying to break it before it gets too strong.[61] It will be hard to do; it has existed for six years now, and is well rooted. All this trouble is making the farmers more determined than ever, and many more farmers joined up this year. It is a co-operative system, and I'm very interested. Each little district has their own little Union, and I have just recently been elected secretary of our local, and besides, I have been made Wheat Pool canvasser. I get $2.50 for every new member, and I help fill in his contract. You may think that I have enough to do without getting mixed up in such matters when I'm thinking of moving away soon, but I think it may do me a lot of good in days to come. All this work will give me a good reference with the Wheat Pool managers and thus may give me my daily bread later on.

At present I am busy selling all that I have here, and it looks like I will be able to breathe a little freer in a couple of weeks time. I have talked with my bank manager [*Pat Mahoney?*], and he thinks it is best for me to sell my outfit now, if I can get a reasonable price for it, but in a couple of weeks I'll be able to give you all the details. [*In 1973, father added*: *The bank manager*] said times are going to get worse instead of better for a long time.

Dear Brother-Teacher! When you write me again, tell me a little about what they think of our "Pool" in Denmark. If you hear about anybody who is thinking of emigrating to Canada, tell them it is better to stay at home. In the end, let me tell you that I am, as usual, in good health and optimistic, and much better off than 70 percent of the Canadian farmers, even if I'm almost broke.

Lots of love to all of you,

from Helge

---

[61] The Grain Exchange would buy the farmers' wheat in the fall, then sell it later, profiting if the price went up. The Wheat Pool would buy on installments, sharing any profits earned later. But in 1929, the price of grain went down so fast that the first payment was already too much. Close to bankruptcy, the Wheat Pool was bailed out by Provincial Government.

[*Diary*:] Wed., March 19, 1930. Much has happened the last two months. I am trying to sell my farm. I have a buyer. I am asking $300 cash and $450 next fall. They are hard times over here. On April 15, I have to pay $226 on my car, and I have no money. I am also thinking of letting the car go. I can save a lot of money if I sell it now. I have been elected secretary of Indian Spring Wheat Pool local and am canvassing for the Wheat Pool. I have spent a bit of time getting new Pool members but have had a hard time with it. Ed Wall is staying with me these days. He is broke and cannot go any place. Today we have a violent snowstorm.
Tues., March 25, 1930. Had letters from both Inge and Gudde [*cousins in Denmark, daughters of Vilhelm*]. Got Inge's first and answered hers first. All the time I thought that I had a buyer for my outfit, but he backed out Sunday. Was at Hussar yesterday with Ross who paid all expenses. Sold my car to Mr. French, the bank teller. Still getting several chances to sell. Worked for Calgary Light Power yesterday p.m. Made $2.
Shepard, [*now part of east Calgary*] May 10, 1930. The situation looked too threatening, so I sold my outfit to Old Ross. Sold my radio to Earl Bryant. Had some difficulty getting some solid work, but finally got a job with Walter Schang again.

Now I have forgotten to write in the diary again, so I have to try to remember far back. As spring moved closer, I got more and more agitated. I had to meet a debt of $226 for the new car and had no money; I had to plow 180 acres and had no fodder for my horses; the price of wheat stayed down; we did not get our cheque from the Wheat Pool. All in all, the outlook was very miserable.

Then one day I made a quick decision. I wanted to sell my outfit and go to work again. It took me a long time to find a reliable buyer; three different families wanted it, but I was afraid they would not be able to pay me. So finally I sold to Old Ross for $750. He got everything except my radio, blankets and instruments. After that I sold my radio to Earl Bryant. Because I owed money at Hussar, I got $200 cash from Ross and a note for the $550 for October 1. Then I paid what I owed at Hussar and drove to Calgary because I had heard that Walter Schang was there.

I found Walt, but he could not promise a job because he had already hired Art Nickle, but he would do his best, and that was all I could expect. So he promised to let me know within two weeks what he could do for me. So I went back to Hussar again, and here I sold my car to the bank teller, Harold French, for $450. I played at a dance at Wintering Hills and told them it was the last time I would play there. It was really fun to see how many friends I had acquired, and we had a tremendously fine good-bye dance.

I went home with Lloyd Heaton that night and stayed there until next day.[62] From there I went over to Earl Bryant's where I stayed for about a week during which I helped Earl. One night Lyle Tonneson came together with Miss Pugh and told me that Walter Schang had phoned for me and that I had to meet him as soon as possible. So the next morning Earl drove me over to McKinney, and he took me to Hussar in his car. When I came to Hussar, I had hoped to see Walt, but I had no luck.

Finally, I telephoned McKinnon in Calgary where he was staying and learned that Walter was in Calgary and would like to see me there. I asked them to meet me at the Empress Hotel the next day at 5 p.m. Saw Harold at the bank and the grocer, Hans M. [*Madsen*], and I drove in Harold's car, a trip of 200 miles for the rest of the day. We saw East Coulee, Wayne, Drumheller, Rosedale, Rosebud and Standard. A wonderful trip. I slept at Hans's that night. The next morning, I took the Calgary bus. At 5 p.m. I met Walt as planned, but since it had rained and snowed all day, he said we had to wait until it cleared up. I met Art Nickle who had arrived already, and we got together and went to all the theatres and dances, etc., while we were waiting for the weather to clear. Finally, on Good Friday, it cleared up. Then we drove out to Airdrie, sixteen miles north, to pick up the plows, etc., and we drove out here to Shepard where Walt had a job breaking a section of prairie.[63]

It took us two days to move all that machinery. After that we drove to Hussar where his Caterpillar 60 stood together with

---

[62] Lloyd Heaton, then age twenty-two, was living and working on his father's farm, a few miles southeast of father's place. Born in Carstairs, Alberta, he had moved to Washington State and then came to the Hussar district in 1920 with his family.

[63] The land Walter Schang's outfit (with father) plowed, east side of Section 29, Tp. 22, R. 28, near Shepard—east of Calgary—was the last unbroken, unfenced section in that part of the country. Professionally photographed, the event caused quite a stir in the community. Using a 60 caterpillar and an eight bottom breaking plow, they broke, disced and fenced the land that summer. The land had been bought in 1903 by a brother of William Plaspohl in Indiana. Walter Schang's brother, Eugene (Gene), came to Canada in 1929, leased the land, married, and farmed until he retired.

Breaking the Last Virgin Prairie—Ole operating plows, Eugene Schang on caterpillar. Shepard, Alberta, 1930.

his road outfit. He started up the tractor and pulled a bunk car and a cook car the sixty miles to Shepard. Art and Gene (Walt's brother) drove the tractor. It was terribly cold while we moved, and we had a hard trip. When we reached Shepard, we took the tractor apart and fixed it up for the summer. It took two days. After that we started plowing, and we plowed the 640 acres in 13 ½ days and nights. Art drove the cat at night and had a new man at the plows. Gene drove during the day, and I was on the plow. We get along fine. We have finished now and are waiting for a road job.

Fri., May 16, 1930. A couple of days ago, we were ordered to move to Hussar to fix the [*road*] grades, so we managed to get here without great difficulty. That is to say, on the way up here, Art drove too close to the ditch, and we overturned the hayrack full of coal, machinery & junk. When the rack overturned, the shaft broke. I sat on the tractor with Art, and neither of us felt anything until we had gone a quarter mile and Andy Anderson drove by us in his truck and stopped and asked if we knew we had overturned the wagon. Then we had to drive back, and at that time Walt and Gene had arrived in Walt's truck. It took us all evening to fix it.

Tues., May 20, 1930. We finally got the grades fixed and today have started grading the road five miles from Hussar to Moffat's. Last Friday we moved out to Moffat's. I am handy man and rock picker. Art on the Cat, Walt on the first grader and Gene on the second.

Sat., May 24, 1930. We finished that road and moved from Moffat's out to Treacy's.[64] When we moved out from Moffat's yard, Art made too sharp a turn and broke a "reach" on the kitchen car. It took us an hour to fix it. Today there will be a stampede at Hussar, but we will not stop for that. This afternoon we have graded from Treacy's back to where we had stopped before. I am on the back grader now and am doing quite all right.

Sun., June 8, 1930. At the moment, we are at Dalum, a Danish colony. We have finished ten miles from Wayne to Clark's. While we were grading that road, they were celebrating the Danish Constitutional Day at the colony and had a dance at a schoolhouse far from our camp. I went to that dance and had a great time and got to know a whole lot of new people, among others many nice, Danish girls. I also saw Godfrey Nielsen [*a Danish farmer, northwest of Hussar*].[65] He told me that he had seen Emily many times and understood from her that she did not realize why I had stopped seeing her. I told him why, and he thought I had done the right thing. He says he can see she is still in love with me. Poor girl! Oh bother, what am I to do about it? It is awfully dry here in this district. Many acres of wheat land have blown away and are bare. It does not look well for the farmers if we do not get some rain soon. I am certainly happy that I sold my farm.

Sun., June 15, 1930. Have moved up to Earl Johnson's now.[66] Monday we moved up near Rosebud and graded two miles. Now we have a job here of fifteen miles. Friday and Saturday, there was a violent wind, and following that quite a bit of rain. Friday morning we started out, but only did about a mile when the storm became too much. Wind and rain and dust into your face so you could not stand it. Today the weather is fine, so because we are

---

[64] Willard Treacy arrived in Alberta from St. Mary's, Ontario, in 1906. As a youth, he worked at various ranches in southern Alberta until he landed at the Treend ranch where he met Lily Treend. Marrying in 1913, they farmed near her parents' place, and, in 1935, bought a ranch near Dorothy as well. They had nine childen.

[65] Godfrey and Stanza Nielsen were born in Copenhagen, Denmark, emigrating to the Standard-Hussar area as young adults—where they met. Returning to Denmark to live after marriage, they later came back, farming north of Hussar.

[66] Earl Johnson came to the Hussar district with his parents and family from Kansas in 1916, enticed by CPR land agents. In 1924 he and his brother, Jay—both bachelors at the time—leased a farm about eight miles north of Hussar. By 1930 they had gone separate ways, as Earl could see that mechanization was going to take over agriculture, while Jay preferred farming with horses.

only a few miles from Vera and Ernie, I went over there to find out how Emily is doing. Vera has had a baby and has had to have help most of the summer. Vera told me that Emily had become angry with Dr. Spankie and stopped going there even though her ears are still full of pus. She has been to a Chinese doctor who has given her some lozenges for her back. But how will that help her ears? I asked Vera to remember me to her. That is all I can do about it.

Mon., June 16, 1930. Today Walter sent me to Calgary in the truck for some parts for the plow. I left here at 6 in the morning. Was there at 9:30. On the way home, I met the Petersens who stood by the side of the road with a soft tire on their Studebaker. I stopped and helped them. Emily was in the car. She told me that she felt better.[67]

On the way home, I stopped at Hussar where I saw Mr. Reesor. He has been to the doctor and is not supposed to work for a whole year. Mrs. Reesor told me that Emily had become engaged to Matt [*Stanton*] and was going to marry in the fall. He is supposed to make $300 a month???! Returned at 1 p.m. Was on the grader in the afternoon. A very strong wind blew today. The price of wheat is $1.00 5/8 a bushel. The price went down 16 cents the last week.

Wed., July 3, 1930. The last while we have had lots of rain, and the wheat looks good all over. We have had to stop many days and

Emily Petersen beside the family's Studebaker, Standard, 1929.

[67] It was a decisive moment. Later in life, father mentioned this incident a number of times, saying how "very pretty" she had looked that day and how attracted he was to her again.

made very slow progress. Last Saturday I went to a dance at Wintering Hills. Camping at Andy Brown's.[68]

July 20 to 30, 1930. We are up at Dave Cyr's.[69] We have been to the Calgary Stampede (I spent $70). We (Art & Alfred and I) had an excellent trip. We saw everything there was to see, and that was a great deal. We were also up in the Crystal Swimming Pool; here I met, among others, Olive Barrier, a little French girl with whom I had some fun a couple of years ago. We renewed our friendship. She is a sales woman at T-Eatons. We were also down at the Palliser Hotel on the Friday for the big cowboy-ball. That was fun. On Sunday we went to Bowness Park where we took a canoe and had a wonderful tour up through the canals. After we had been out for some time, they started playing at a concert in a pavilion on an island in the water. At 10 o'clock, we wanted to go back into the city and had a hard time because there were hundreds of people.

A good job until Provincial funding ran out—the Schang road crew, Ole Nissen on last grader. Hussar area, 1930.

---

[68] Andy Brown grew up in Scotland, married and homesteaded near Milk River, and leased the Hawkeye Ranch land in 1923.

[69] Dave Cyr had a ranch near Dorothy, raising first cattle, then sheep. Eventually he moved northwest to the bush country.

September 30, 1930. Am at Majorville [*southeast of Gleichen*]. In the meantime, Walt has bought an old 45 cat-tractor, and Gene and I have been up to Shepard disc breaking. When we finished, we drove the Brown tractor down here to Majorville, and we work on the road with both tractors. Have had a letter from home recently. They are not happy with me, and I am getting a little angry and wrote back that I am capable of looking after myself. The price of wheat is down to 48 cents; am happy I do not have wheat to sell this year.
October 20, 1930. Have not worked for a couple of days. We have had a violent snowstorm, and the frost has made the ground so hard that you cannot dig into it. I guess it is getting to be the end of it. I am thinking of going to school this winter.

My mother, Emily Petersen, kept a diary in 1930. All that year she had gone for periodic visits to Calgary for ear treatments. Though father wrote on November 16—the previous year—that he had broken up with her, she told of receiving a letter from him in January and another with photos in February. But after the break-up she began corresponding with Matt Stanton, Petersens' former hired man. The son of an eastern dentist, Stanton had come west for a harvesting job in 1928. In March he was back at the Petersens', and he and mother became engaged. That summer they went on a holiday to see his relatives in British Columbia where he stayed for a road job at Bull River, the same place where father had worked earlier.

Returning to Standard, mother wrote on June 16, "Walter, Dad, and I went to Calgary. On the way we had a flat tire. Ole Nissen was coming from Shepard, so he helped us fix it. It was the first time I had seen him since he quit me on August 31, 1929. My ears were getting better...."

Emily and Matt Stanton, British Columbia, 1930.—Courtesy the Petersen families

By August, Matt had gone north to Spirit River to look for

a homestead. Mother bought her wedding dress and accessories, and was given gifts. But by October, Matt was back on the prairies, with no homestead and no money, and the wedding was postponed—to grandmother's satisfaction. Matt telegraphed his parents for money, and on getting it, he left for the east. On December 30, mother received a letter from him, but she did not reveal the contents. The next day, she and her brother, Walter, went to the Hussar New Year's dance where father was playing with the orchestra. "We had a nice time," she wrote, "Hussar orchestra played. Enough said."

1931

Whenever he was out of work, father could always appeal to Walter Schang. But things had changed. Walter had met May McKinnon, a young teacher from the Bow River area, at a school-house dance, and they had married in 1929. Shortly afterwards, May contracted cancer, and Walter nursed her through an eight-month illness until she died, losing their child as well. It "tore him up so badly" that Walter sold the farm north of Hussar and moved southwest to the Shepard area, where he continued with his contracting business, mostly breaking land, plowing, and threshing. After this, Walter would only need seasonal help.

[*Diary*:] Calgary, February 7, 1931. Have been in Calgary since last November. All I've done is feed my face and lose money in the stock market. It's been a long and dreary winter. Just lately things have cheered up a little when Emmie wrote me, and we had a reunion.

[*Calgary*] Monday, April 6, 1931
Dear Gudrun and Alfred!

It is a long time since last you heard from me! Yes! I'm still alive! I had actually planned on coming home on a visit, but the plans didn't turn out; instead I went and got married! Well, it shouldn't be such a surprise to you—I'm old enough.

Emily and I were married last Thursday, April 2nd. At the present time we have a room in Hotel Wales, which to us is "seventh heaven." Emily is now over her sickness, and as we decided that life would be empty without each other, we got married. Emily is still somewhat hard-of-hearing, but the doctor has assured her that the hearing will gradually become better. So now we travel life's road together. We realize that life will not be a bed of roses, but we will face it together. It looks like I will be working for Walter Schang during the summer; so we can get some money scraped together, but it is our plan to get a small farm as soon as possible.

So many loving greetings and hopes that you are all well, from your new sister-in-law,

Emily, and Helge

Standard, Alta., May 17, 1931
Dear Gudrun and Alfred!

Many thanks for your letter and the $15! It was a wonderful surprise. We appreciate your good wishes for the future. We still have the money, but we have decided what we will use it for—we will purchase a nice linoleum, which we need badly, and we can get a real nice one for the $15. Believe me, $15 is a lot of money over here, right now. Emily is staying with her folks this summer, while I am working on road construction gang. We are quite optimistic that we will find a small farm this fall, and make a home for ourselves. All our possessions are stored with Emily's folks, and we have nearly everything we need for our new home. Times are very, very hard over here, but surely, better times must come soon? I've been staying with Emily's folks for a week, but must go back to work tomorrow. But as the outfit moves so often from place to place, I believe it will be best if you address your letters here to Standard, and Emily can forward them to me when they arrive.

I earn $90 a month including board & room, and that is a lot more than I could get on a farm the last few years. We knew that it would be very hard to live apart, but we are prepared to face circumstances, as long we have each other. Let nobody convince you that we were forced to get married! But the more we are together, the more we love each other. Emily's hearing is about the same, but I'm so used to it that I don't notice that I have to speak a little louder for her to hear.

Emily is of Danish origin, but her parents came from South Jutland, and she doesn't understand high Danish, but I'll teach her soon. Their dialect is very strange to me, so we speak English all the time. I'll finish for now—again many thanks for your letter and present. Lots of love to our little nieces,

Emily and Helge

1932

*Father still had not received full payment from Louis Ross, the man who had bought his farm, and who was also likely suffering from the Depression. Mother wrote in her diary on February 13: "Ole walked down [*from Standard*] to Ross's at Dorothy to see if he could get some things for his money." Six days later, father was back with three horses, harness and machinery. Then they began packing. The Provincial Government was offering a two-third discount on fares, helping farmers in drought-ridden southern Alberta to move further north to "the sticks," as my parents called it. Many farmers took advantage of this, including my parents, moving to Caroline, west of Red Deer.*

Standard, February 5, 1932
Dear Gudrun and Alfred!

Finally you are getting a letter from Canada, and first I thank you so sincerely for your Christmas letter. Really, there was a good reason for my long silence, and I shall try to explain the reason. When Emily and I were married last year, the future looked quite bright for us. I was assured of a good job with the road construction crew, but the luck was against us—there was no more money in the provincial treasury to continue with the roadwork. The money granting relief to the farmers had disappeared during the winter. As a result, I was forced to look for work elsewhere, and as the times were very bad, I found it hard to get other work. By the time I finally found work, the most of my earnings had disappeared. Emily was forced to stay with her parents. So, there was not much to write home about.

By November 15th I was laid off, and I went back to Standard, where I stayed with Emily's parents the most of the winter. We were not very satisfied with living off Emily's parents, and during December and January I kept looking for a farm. So that you can understand conditions over here, I must describe our difficulties in Alberta. The last three or four years there has been a severe shortage of rainfall. And as a result, the soil is very dry—there is no sub-soil moisture at all, the topsoil is like powder, and the wind blows it around in great clouds. Emily's parents have not had a crop the last three years, and things are getting tough, even for them, though they are out-of-debt—as far as lands and buildings are concerned. Under ordinary circumstances, they would have nothing to worry about.

About 200 miles northwest from Standard, there lies a totally different country. It is bush country, where the farms are very small compared to the prairie country. Most farms are 160 or 320 acres bush land, with 25 to 50 acres broken to farm land. It is hard work to clear the land of trees and brush, but it rains a lot there as the land lies close to the mountains, so they are always sure of a good crop, with plenty of vegetables in the cellar. It costs very little to live there. The big drawback with this country is the distance to the railroad, but CPR is talking about building a road right through this land.

So I went up to the country and bought 160 acres of which 25 acres are broken for farming. There are three good springs on the quarter, with the best water one could wish for. I say bought, but actually I rent the land for two years, with an option to buy it for $1,200. So it will be an opportunity for us to see if we like it. There is a fair house on the land, with several outbuildings and a lot of trees with which we can build more. We do not pay taxes on the land, and can keep all that we raise. The owner is a returned soldier, who gets a small pension, as he is not able to do any work. If we like it there, we have first chance to buy it for $1,200. Since we were married, we have gathered quite a lot of equipment, things we will need to start farming. And I still have $325 coming from the man I sold my horses and machinery to, and I can purchase four horses, a cow and much other needed equipment from him. Emily owns a cow, three calves, some chickens and a lot of needed household goods, so luckily it will not cost much to set up our housekeeping. It will cost us quite a lot to move onto the land. We will have to live very sparingly during the summer, but we are not afraid. We hope to get by until times get better, and at least we will be together. I plan on moving up about March 1st, so I will give you our new address. It may look like I'm not interested in writing to you, but facts are that I hate to write about bad luck, and we have surely had a lot of that the last year.

Still, I'm glad that I let the farm at Dorothy go; the drought made conditions unbearable there. Be sure I think about you many, many times, and like to hear from you. I have a 100 percent farm wife, and we feel that we can survive until the good times come again. When summer comes, we will try and take some pictures of our new farm. Will you be so kind, and let the rest of the family know about us, so that I don't need to write to each of them? Five cents today is worth as much as a dollar was two years ago.

Best wishes to ALL from

Helge

Caroline, November 19, 1932
Dear Gudrun and Alfred!

First I must thank you very much for your birthday letter; it is very touching that you still remember my birthday. You asked me if I received the two books you sent over last Spring. Yes, I did, and many thanks; those and Vilhelm's papers [*Vilhelm, father's older brother, captain of a ferry from Denmark to Germany*] were the first Danish I had read for a long time. I don't blame you if you figured that I didn't care much about them, but I did! The reason I did not thank you was the fact that I would have to tell you how we were getting along. To tell the truth, it has been nothing to write home about!

It took most of our money to get moved to Caroline. And by the time we got settled, it started to rain, and it rained for two solid weeks. The log house we live in leaked in many places, and we had to move things around to keep them dry. It kept raining off and on during the whole summer, the soil was soaked the most of the time, and the weather did not get warm enough to allow a good growth on the land. Therefore our harvest was very poor. Down on the prairie, where there had been drought for four years, the rain came in just the right time for them to get a bumper harvest. It's too bad that a person cannot foresee the future!

However, during the summer we lived on what butter and eggs we could trade for groceries. We could see that there would not be much wheat to sell, so if we wanted money to live on during the winter, we would have to go down to the prairie to earn some money. I therefore arranged with a neighbour to look after our farm. I borrowed some money for travel expenses, and here I am, on the prairie again.

We arrived about August 1st, and I helped my brother-in-law [*Herman*] during his harvest. At threshing time, I ran his separator—for a job that three years ago paid $12 per day, I got $3.50 per day. It has been poor weather for harvesting, just a few good days harvest weather, then the rain came, with no sunshine to dry the stooks. Finally, the snow came to put an end to the harvest. There is about 25 percent of wheat still standing in the fields. We can't wait any longer; we must get back to tend our horses and cattle before the winter sets in proper. We have bought an old Ford car (for $7!), and we are returning the first decent day that comes. It is a distance of 180 miles from here. I can just see Alfred's face when you read this letter. Where is the future for us? I can't say for sure, but if good times come back to the land, we will make it somehow! Compared to 75 percent of the farmers in this land, we are free-of-debt. So many farms are sold for taxes, and every cent they earn goes to pay old debts, no matter where they try to sell their grain.

Father-in-law has just sold two carloads of wheat. He received 25½ cents a bushel. It cost him 7½ cents a bushel to get it harvested, 5 cents to get it cut and stooked. Last year he didn't even have seed wheat, so he got Government assistance—he got 400 bushels of wheat at a price of 47 cents a bushel. This fall the Government is the first that has to be repaid before the elevators can give him any money for his own use. All loans bear 7 percent interest. He had to buy fodder for his horses and cattle more than a year ago, until the rains finally came last summer to make the grass green again. So despite having a great big harvest with 10,000 bushels of wheat, there will be very little left by the time he pays up his debts.

There is a lot of talk nowadays about an important Imperial Conference in Ottawa. There were great hopes that something would come out of it, but it turned out to be all propaganda, and the farmers and workers are now getting together, trying to organize themselves. Maybe they can get some results? Meanwhile, with a bit of luck during the next few years, we are getting quite a little herd of cattle. Though at present they are not worth much money, still we believe it is at least something to face the future with.

Really, we live in a beautiful country [*at Caroline*]: it is, of course, mostly trees and meadows. There are three springs on our farm. They join and make a three foot stream that runs right by our house. The house is a log house. I might as well tell you that we just could not afford to take any pictures the last couple of years. The last little while it has been just like a holiday, with beautiful sunshine, no wind nor dust storms. The air is full of scent from the flowers. A short distance from our home flows the river "Raven," where there is good fishing. I have one objection with this country—it is about 4,000 ft. above sea level, and is subject to frost in the fall.

I'm thinking about Emily—her hearing is no better! When we are together at home, I hardly notice it, but when we are with strangers, it is quite a handicap for her. She has a $55 hearing aid, but of course that costs money for batteries, etc., and it is somewhat awkward for her as she has to hold the apparatus in one hand. After New Year we may get her another hearing test.

We have now been married for 1½ years, and it is said that it happens in the best of families, so I may have some more news for you soon. Maren Johanne writes and tells us that Johannes. [*father's youngest brother, a blacksmith*] has suggested that the reason I don't come home for a visit is the fact that I'm too hard up! That wasn't the reason a few years ago, but it is now. Now, don't think that we are dressed in rags, that we go hungry or live on Government welfare. Far from it.

I believe it will be close to Christmas by the time you get this letter, so I wish you all a merry X-mas and a happy New Year. Should your thoughts drift over to Canada this coming season, they will meet mine on their way to Denmark.

Love to All from

Helge and Emily

Towards the end of his life, father mentioned the following letter, saying it was the hardest he had ever written.

Caroline, Alta., December 9, 1932

Dear Gudrun and Alfred!

It is only a short while ago since I sent you my last letter, so I'm sure you will be surprised to receive this second letter. To tell the truth, I've been wanting to write you for the last week, but I could not seem to express my needs to write you. However, to start with, I cannot see how we are going to make out this winter; and if possible, I beg you to try and see if you could send us some money. We have our back against the wall, and I do not know what we can do when Emily has to go to the hospital next March 1st. It will cost us $50 cash before she can come home again. To get the doctor to come out here will cost us $35, and the doctor says that she should go to the hospital, as she has not completely recovered from her sickness of a couple of years ago.

When last I wrote you, everything looked pretty good. We bought the old Ford car for half the cost of the return to our farm. But by the time we got here, we had experienced a lot of trouble and expense. We had to buy a new tire and tube; our expenses were twice what we could have travelled for. Still it is not all bad; now I'll have a car to get Emily to the doctor if it becomes necessary. However, the worst that happened was the mess the man who was supposed to look after the farm had left for us!

He had left the crop standing in the field, now soaked with snow. The horses and cattle were not taken care of and had broken down a lot of fences. They got into the grain field and had tramped most of the grain down. When he finally got around to haul the crop in, he threw it up on top of the flat-roofed barn. There it lay, all in great heaps for rain and snow to further deteriorate what was left. One-half of the ducks and geese have disappeared; and all I could do was to give him a good piece of my mind. Now I'll have to buy feed for over half of the winter.

I had a horse that went lame last summer. When the snow came, it could not find any feed. The man let it wander around until it finally died. I was not so well acquainted here in this country. I'd had quite a lot to do with this man; he is a thirty-year-old bachelor and appeared quite responsible when we worked together. He moved his things over in our house and lived here while we were gone. I now have no seed grain, but that is not the worst.

It is on account of Emily that I'm writing you—she has got to have good care in the days to come. So now you are my last hope. See if you can spare me a few dollars; talk to the rest of the family and ask them too. I know that times are hard for you folks too, but I beg of you to see what you can do. I have lost all my self-esteem, and can only think about Emily's welfare. If you can help us, keep track of the money, and I will repay you as soon as I can. If we can hang on to what we now have, we might have a hope for the future. I can see now that we could have stayed on the prairie, but it is too late for "after-thoughts."

Hoping to hear from you soon, I send best regards to all,
from yours sincerely,

Helge

[*Diary*:] December 28, 1932. Made a stoneboat. Cut wood. Cleaned barns. Clarke [*landlord*] was up to get his pork. He seemed willing to pay for 1,000 feet of lumber [*probably for a new house*]. Nice weather.

December 29, 1932. Went with Alleson for load of straw. Stopped in town for mail & groceries. Put up notice about playing for dances. Mrs. Langley wants me to teach her grandson the violin. The folks [*Petersens*] sent us $5. Emmie's Rag-Rug (premiums) arrived.

1933

In 1933 the Great depression began its fourth year. Conditions in Caroline were in some ways harder than those in Standard-Hussar, prompting father and mother to return that year to the parched plains. This was a pattern often repeated by others—moving away from the drought, then moving back to the prairies, and sometimes leaving again.

[*Diary*:] January 2, 1933. Young Brown boy came up to borrow a Ford ignition coil. Told him I'd want it in February. In the afternoon, Campbell [*a neighbour*] brought us some pork he owed us.
January 3, 1933. Cleaned barns. Took Pete [*horse*] and hauled in some firewood. Cut wood. Cold weather now.
January 4, 1933. Got a few groceries & mail. Got a letter from Alfred. Stopped at Brown's and talked about getting Elsie to take a few lessons on the violin.
January 5, 1933. Went out and shot a few rabbits.
Fri., January 6, 1933. Cut wood. Emmie washed clothes Saturday.
Mon., January 7, 1933. Went to the Young Peoples' meeting in the evening. Played on the violin & accordion, but don't know if that will ever do me any good. Got a package with books from Alfred. Took white-faced heifer to Langley's bull.
Sun., January 8, 1933. Went over to the Campbells' for dinner. They gave us two sacks of wheat for interest for the $10 [*owed to my parents-in-law*].
Mon., January 9, 1933. Had an awful blizzard in the morning.
Tues., January 10, 1933. Campbells came over to make a deal with us for the old cow. They'd only give us 10 bushels wheat for her. But they changed it to 15 bushels oats and 5 bushels wheat. We told them we'd think it over.
Wed., January 11, 1933. Made up our minds to let Campbell have the cow. I took it over, but they'd changed their mind. Wrote a letter to Alfred.
Thurs., January 12, 1933. Sold the old cow to Shur for what we owed him & three sacks of chop. They came and got her.

Caroline, Alta., January 11, 1933
Dear Gudrun and Alfred!

Thank you very much for your Christmas letter, and a few days later I received the package with books. Believe me, we were glad to get them! Emily cannot ask enough about the islands around

Fyn since she saw all the pictures. There are several pictures of places that I know from Denmark. Niels Hald's books I read right away, and they gave me much to think about. Have I used the proper opportunity life has offered me through life? That is the question I often ask myself, especially these days, when all seems so hopeless. When I assess my life, I've been in Canada nearly ten years, and what progress have I made? Not much. I'm getting older and more careful (too careful). I have tried to save so I could farm for myself; maybe I should have used that money to study radio and electricity, so I could get in position to have a better way of life? If I had known then what I know now, you can bet your boots that I would have done something different.

The worst of it is that I love the land! It seems that I must have the fresh air, sunshine and animals around me. If anybody was made for a farmer's life, that's me. When I started farming at Dorothy, the farmer's life was good, and I had hopes that a few years would see me in good shape. But it turned out otherwise. We were hit by the drought. When Emily and I started up again, we chose a slower, but to us, safer plan by the way of mixed farming. But it is tough for us, with prices forever going down and no place to find extra work. We might have made it, if we had had a few more cattle.

Here is another of fortune's quirks: we own a couple of heifers, old enough to have a calf, but it has been impossible for us through summer and fall to get them with calf. There appears to be a sickness among cattle which prevents them from pregnancy up here as well as on the prairie. We have tried a number of bulls, but we had hoped to be able to milk the cows in the spring. As it is, we will have no milk until September, unless we can get a milk cow somehow. I've been trying to make a deal with a man who has owed us some money for some time. But it is not easy.

It seems like nobody pays their debts these days. The large oil and machine companies are writing off all interest and will take wheat as payment at a price of 35 cents to 40 cents over the market price, just so the accounts can be written off their books. They are not having much luck! The trouble is that no one can raise wheat for the prices of the present market. Still, we must prepare for the next year. God only knows what will be the end of it all!

Alfred asks if I do much hunting? All I have is a 22 rifle, but I do shoot lots of rabbits and partridges for food. We often eat moose and deer meat, which we get from the real hunters. About fifteen or twenty miles west of here, there is a lot of big game, such as moose, deer, elk and bears. I'm looking forward to going along on a hunt if ever I can afford to buy a rifle. There are not many wild geese or ducks, because we do not have many lakes in this district; they fly on down to the prairie. However, we do quite a lot of fishing, we are only a couple of miles from a river, and we go there often during the summer. Lots of fish there. We still have a camera, and as soon as we can afford to buy film, we will take some pictures next summer and send you some.

In closing I can tell you that Emily's fine and sends you lots of love. Me also, to the whole family, from yours truly,

Helge

Caroline, Alta., January 31, 1933
Dear Alfred!

We have just received your letter with $50 enclosed; the letter was dated January 3rd. Thank you so very, very much! We shall never forget your goodness and generosity. Your letter gave me much to think about. Also, thanks for the newspaper clipping. I can see that it is just as hard to get started farming in Denmark as it is here, especially if one goes in debt right from the start.

Emily [*seven months pregnant*] is feeling pretty good, and we are now prepared to cope with the situation. We are, of course, still a little nervous; it is forty miles to the hospital. And we do not know what time the trip will come, and the roads are often very poor. Cars drive between Caroline and Innisfail, but if a sudden snowstorm comes, the road will be very bad. It can get blocked for several days. It is impossible to drive a car the three miles from our farm to Caroline, so I have arranged it so that I can load the car on a sleigh and haul it to Caroline. We now hope for the best; I have done all that I can. I will, of course, write you as soon as it is over.

And now about your offer to extend us further help. I shall never forget your generosity—for you and Vilhelm to guarantee a loan on my behalf—but I cannot see where we have a right to take advantage of such an offer, especially during these uncertain times. I never dreamed that such an offer would come. I could see that some help was necessary when Emily's parents were unable to help us with cash money.

Meanwhile, it doesn't look very good for us up in this country. The price of butter and eggs is ridiculously low, so is the price of pigs, while conditions on the prairie have recovered a lot. We now wish that we had stayed down there. It is easy enough to know when it is too late. We might move down there again next spring. I am dealing with a neighbour of father-in-law's about taking charge of his farm, that is, using his horses and tractor to farm his land. As my wages, I would get all I can raise on eighty acres of summerfallow plus $10 a month to live on. The cash money will be deducted from the proceeds of the eighty acre crop. Nothing is sure as yet; I'm trying to get a little better deal. As for me farming in Denmark, I know so very little of the way of farming there, and I would only be a burden to the family. It would also be a shame to borrow money to come back to Denmark. You ask me if I have written to Lex? I promised that I would, but I can't make myself do it. Lex has shown a lot of interest in me, but he has always advocated that I quit farming and start in some other line. And I'm afraid that he is hurt because I have not taken his advice.

I'm teaching a few kids to play with a local dance orchestra, but I'm afraid to leave Emily alone. But I hope times will be better all over. Once again, many thanks and I hope that you won't worry too much about us. We are sure that we will get by somehow.

Best regards,

Helge

P. S. Emily also sends you greetings and thanks. Everything came as a surprise for her.

Standard, March 26, 1933
Dear Alfred and Gudrun!

This evening I am rushing this letter off to you, because today at 3:20 p.m. Emily gave birth to a 7½ lb. boy, and he has a very healthy squeal, too! Of course, he already has a name: Norman Koenig Nissen. After all, I'm still proud of the old family name.

It all sounds easy enough, but believe me, many things have happened since last I wrote. First, my brother-in-law [*Herman*] came to visit us; he had hardly set his foot inside the door when it started to snow. The storm lasted three days, and when it was over the roads were completely blocked. That started us worrying, and we decided to move down to Standard. Emily and her brother took the train, after I had hauled them the forty miles to Innisfail with the sleigh. I had a little stove in the sleigh, and a tent over us. It took us all day to get to Innisfail, and the whole next day for me to get back again.

After that I was busy getting ready to move our outfit to Standard. I had five horses, four of which I hitched to a hayrack, three cows, ducks, turkeys, a cat and a dog. I sold all the chickens as I was afraid they would freeze on the way down. I sold a good deal of the machinery and left the Ford car, a stove and a few other things. (I will pick them up in the summer.) I loaded the hayrack, and started on my way, a distance of 180 miles.

The first fifty miles, I used the sleigh; the rest of the way, I had to use the wagon, as the snow disappeared. It didn't take long before the cows gave up, and I had to load them on the hayrack, until finally the horses played out. So I had to unload the cows again, and they made it the rest of the way. It took me eight days to make the trip. It was a hard and trying trip, more so for one man alone. Towards evening, when I tried to stop at a farm, I often had to go another mile or so before I found a farmer who would let me stop overnight. And all the time I was worrying about Emily, because the doctor had estimated her confinement at no later than March 2nd. However, I finally reached Standard, and I have been here ten days now.

Mon., 27th.

Here we live only five miles from town, and Emily's folks had the car ready to go. So, when the time came, there wasn't a moment's delay. They say that the boy looks like his father, not that I can notice it; however, he has the high forehead of the Nissen family. Needless to say, I was very proud of him. Emily is doing real well, and when I told her that I was going to write you, she asked me to send you her love. Today I was able, thanks to you, to pay the doctor [*Dr. Fletcher*] $25 and the hospital [*Lee's nursing home*] $25. My in-laws are good Danish people and ready to help us all they can.

As soon as I arrived here, I started to look for a farm to rent, but I haven't had much luck. Father-in-law is willing to let me have some seed wheat and oats for my horses. Meanwhile, I have also been looking for a job as hired man, and the neighbour, a Mr. Lind (Swede) is willing to hire me. He is more of a person of independent means than a poor farmer and owns several pieces of real estate in the USA, so I decided to work for him this summer so I can pay my debt to the Petersens. And for wages he will give me what I can harvest from eighty acres of summerfallow (plowed last year). We will get $10 a month to live off, but that will be taken off my profit at harvest. Father-in-law will use my horses through the summer in return for twenty acres of oats to use as fodder next winter and spring.

Father-in-law has another farm ten miles east of the home farm. He has bought it from CPR, and has paid two installments on it. His older daughter and her husband [*Vera and Ernie Elliott*] have been farming it; but Emily's family has decided to farm the land themselves, along with Emily's two brothers [*Herman and Walter*], so they will have some money for payment to CPR.

His daughter and her husband moved to another farm. But if the folks get a decent crop this year, they have promised that we can rent the farm next year. In any case, Emily & I will move out to the farm after harvest and live there during the winter. Now I hope that you realize that I will pay your loan with the money I earn this summer, before the Canadian dollar goes down.

I will close with all our love,
best regards to everybody at home,

Helge

Standard, May 19, 1933
Dear Gudrun and Alfred!

Many thanks for your letter, dated April 21st. And I thank you very much for the help you have given me with the money. We shall not forget it! And certainly Norman will get his baptismal gift as soon as I can spare it. I can't deny that it's valuable help when all I make in two months is $50. I also thank you for your offer to get started in something at home in Denmark, and I must tell you some of the reasons that I would rather stay here in Canada, at least for a while.

First of all, I cannot face the shame of coming back home, broke. Next, I'm now a married man. Emily is very hard of hearing, and her Danish dialect is very hard to understand. She cannot understand what I tell her in my own Danish. I suppose that difficulty could be overcome in time, but she would miss her mother and Alberta very much. We could, perhaps, face that too, but not when we are broke. Sure, I miss you and the rest of the family at home, and I miss the culture and the kind of life I was used to. I miss our music; as a boy I often said that if I ever got married, it would be to someone who can play the piano. Talk is cheap. Emily does not play the piano; still I would not trade her for the best piano player in Canada. Of course, we often talk about moving to Denmark. She is willing to try it, but we are not willing to be a burden to my family. Things do not look too bright over here, but we must always hope that times will improve soon. The price of wheat has gone up 10 cents in the last month, and we have received a lot of rain. I must close for now because it's late. Emily and the baby are fine, and we send all of you our love. Yours truly,

Helge

1934

By 1934 my parents were leasing a farm, along with some land from the Trust and Guarantee Co., in the Wintering Hills, ten miles north of Hussar. For fuel, father hauled coal from the Comstock mine, twelve miles further north, the only place where it could be bought at 75 cents a load. It was mostly low-grade coal, giving small heat in cold weather but holding fire. For horsemen like father, getting it could be a problem. James Armstrong, a neighbour, tells of setting out at 2 a.m. to arrive ahead of the trucks.[70] *"At times it was heartbreaking when sometimes three trucks or more would speed up behind us, and pass our four-horse teams the last couple of hundred yards, thus making us stand out in the cold an extra three hours longer than necessary to get loaded. Some went the night before and lined up.... Several times I've waited eight hours to get loaded...."*[71]

Chancellor was now my parents' business centre. At Hussar, two years earlier, five businesses and the Masonic Lodge had been completely destroyed by fire, including Clifgard's store, their home above, and all its contents.

Father kept writing in his diary until he got busy in the fields in April. Mother kept a diary, too—continuing throughout their years of farming.

[*Diary*:] Sat., January 6, 1934. Rode over in the Trust & Guarantee to chase out the four Muir horses of Ike's [*horses belonging to Muir*]. In afternoon hauled west granary up to the house. Salem got cut

---

[70] The Chris Armstrong family arrived in the Wintering Hills from Washington in 1919, to farm twelve miles north of Hussar, where their descendants still live. James was one of nine children.

[71] The Hussar Historical Society, *Hussar Heritage*, p. 198.

up a bit, kept him in barn & doctored him with Lysol. Clayton Crory was up for his violin lessons.[72]

Sun., January 7, 1934. Emmie & I dusted all the chickens; afterwards I oiled all the roosts.

Mon., January 8, 1934. Emmie canned beef today. Today Tom Pontec came over and told me I could have a just freshened heifer to milk for feeding it.[73] So I went over with him and got it, also a little month-old pup. Done chores at 10 o'clock. Real nice weather.

Tues., January 9, 1934. Cleaned barn. J.J. [*Petersen*] came over to tell us that they had sold eight ducks for us at Standard.

Wed., January 10, 1934. Killed & dressed eight ducks. Worked till after 11 o'clock p.m. Awful cold wind started up late tonight. Have

Ole and Emily's house from 1934 to spring 1939, ten miles north of Hussar. In the window, Emily's appliquéd flour sack curtains; in foreground, her flowers.

---

[72] Herbert and Edith Crory came from Washington in 1921, farming south of my parents' place. Clayton and Milton, fifteen and thirteen, were two of six children. Clayton paid for most of his lessons by poisoning gophers, digging postholes, hauling coal from the mine, and for much of July 1935, doing heavy field work for 50 cents a day. As an adult, he worked in Idaho mines, and in 1941 he joined the Armed Forces. He was captured by the Japanese in the Philippines where, in 1944, he died in a concentration camp. Milton would farm, raise sheep and become a heavy equipment operator.

[73] A cow is "fresh" when it has just had a calf, and begins producing milk.

a lot of trouble with Pontec's cow. Can't get milk out of one teat. Seems like it has inflammation.

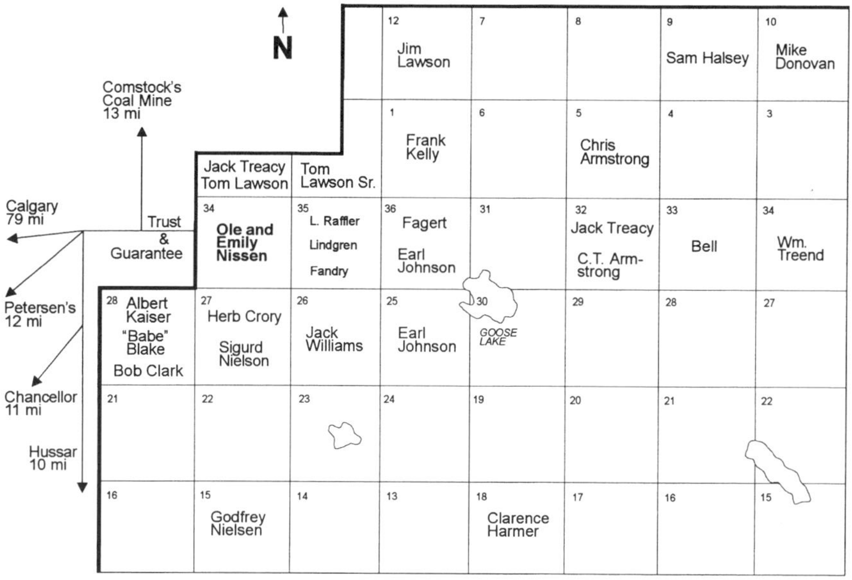

The position of the Nissens' and neighbours' farms, north of Hussar, 1930s. Unspecified are the dates or exact parts of the sections owned or leased. The Nissens also the rented Trust and Guarantee Co. land west of their place. Section numbers are in upper left corners. —Outline of map, and information, courtesy, The Hussar Heritage

Thurs. January 11, 1934. Had to go and get Tom Pontec over to help with the cow. We kept bathing the bag. Later I took the ducks over to J.J., got back at 11 p.m.

Fri., January 12, 1934. Bill Whiteside came over to work on the cow. At night Emmie went with me to Dance at Dahl House. Got back at 5:30 a.m.

Sat., January 13, 1934. Bill Whiteside came over and took the cow back again. Clayton Crory came for his violin lessons.

Sun., January 14, 1934. Herb Crough came over with Crory to make arrangements with me to teach his son, Delbert, the violin.[74]

[74] Croughs lived about seven miles southwest of my folks. Herbert was a WW I veteran who came west in 1919. The parents of his wife Daisy came from Oregon to Hussar, hoping to become wealthy. They got hailed out in 1927, and dried out in the 1930s. Delbert, thirteen in 1934, grew up to be a chartered accountant. Later, father taught his brother, Phillip, who, as an adult, ran a dairy farm and other businesses.

Mon., January 15, 1934. Went to Crory and traded him a turkey hen for a gobbler. Also went to Earl Johnson's to see about some horses. In the afternoon, went to Tom Pontec and got another cow with a calf. She gives a full bucket of milk to a milking; was fresh at Xmas.

Thurs., January 18, 1934. Worked in chicken house, made nests and patched the walls. One egg again.

Fri., January 19, 1934. Was fixing harness. J.J. came over with half a pig all ready for the salt barrel. One egg. Both Emmie & I are feeling sick with a cold. Warm weather but ring around the moon tonight.

Sat., January 20, 1934. Clayton Crory & Delbert Crough were both over for violin lessons. In the evening, I went over to Crory with our gobbler and traded for one of Crory's. Also traded him my accordion for a 2½ year old black saddle mare but didn't bring it home with me.

Sun., January 21, 1934. Emmie left to go and visit J.J.'s. I'm alone with the baby.

January 23, 1934. Had a terrible blizzard. Could hardly face the wind doing chores. The big room was so cold we moved into the kitchen, and at night we moved the bed in the kitchen.

January 25, 1934. At noon found Pete sick in the barn. Emmie & I doctored him. In evening Emmie & I went over and got Crory to see if he knew what to do for Pete. He didn't.

January 26, 1934. Pete still sick. Gave him another dose and turned him loose as he looked better. Sven Ødeland was over and engaged me for dance at Rabbit Lake School [*eight miles northeast of the Nissens*] next Friday. Frank Robey came in evening and stopped here overnight.[75] He went with me to the dance at Dahl House.

January 27, 1934. The boys were here for violin lessons; also Milton Crory brought the little black pony in trade for the accordion. Gave him a lesson. Was supposed to play for dance at Atlas [*school, four miles east*] tonight but didn't go because of bad weather. When it turned nice in the evening, it was too late to go.

January 28, 1934. Chased Ike's horses out of Trust & Guarantee.

---

[75] Frank Robey, a cowboy from the early days, worked for various farmers and ranchers. He lived about fifteen miles southeast of my folks, where he had about thirty head of cattle, some horses and a bit of grassland. He always carried a gun—and a knife, with which he was particularly adept.

January 29, 1934. Fixed harness & cleaned barn & chicken house. Late in afternoon J.J. & mother [*Emily's parents*] came over and stayed with us.
January 31, 1934. J.J. & I went to J. Ingle's sale. I bought a scale and other small things for the house. The roads were a fright with ice.
February 2, 1934. Played for dance at Rabbit Lake school, cleaned up $5.95.
Sat., February 3, 1934. Bob Kelly stopped here today and wanted violin lessons.[76] Made arrangements for Thursday nights. Mr. Ricard & his daughter, Yvette, came to see about lessons on violin. Gave her a lesson.[77] Also Milton Crory & Delbert Crough came for their lessons.
Thurs., February 8, 1934. Went to mine at Comstocks after 1½ tons coal. Tough roads (soft and slippery). Back at 5 p.m. Bob Kelly came for a lesson. Walt & Ernie, Edna Elliott [*Emily's brother and in-laws*] stopped in on the way home from Wayne.
Fri., February 9, 1934. Played for dance at Dahl house.
Sat., February 10, 1934. Most of the day taken up with pupils. Emily visited with Tom Lawsons.[78]
Mon., February 11, 1934. Killed six ducks, took us all day to dress them. In afternoon took heifer calf over to Tom Lawson's and traded it for a buckskin pony. I'm to pay $7.50 to boot. Bought and took home twenty Plymouth Rock chickens at 25 cents apiece. Met Benny Wall at Lawson's. He came back with me and stayed overnight. We picked ducks till 11 p.m. (pin feathers).
February 13, 1934. Took ducks to J.J.'s. Emily & baby went along. Had a long visit until 8 p.m. Got home at 11 p.m. J.J. gave us buggy.

---

[76] Bob Kelly was the twenty-one-year-old son of Frank Kelly, for whom father had worked in June 1924. Bob would later become a chartered accountant in the United States.

[77] Yvette Ricard, age sixteen, came with her parents and three siblings from Quebec in 1918. My folks' neighbours, they farmed nine miles northwest of Hussar. She became a schoolteacher at Shallow Waters, near Hussar.

[78] The Lawsons, neighbours, were originally from Scotland, and were one of the area's first settlers, ranching ten miles north of Hussar. At one time, Tom Lawson Sr. ran some 1,500 head of cattle and 500 horses. By 1919 they had turned mostly to farming, but kept the horses, as the market was good for them until the late 1920s when they were being replaced by tractors. Tom Lawson, then age forty-five, was one of the five children. Married to Nan Pugh, he was a cowboy, a top roper, skilled at breaking horses. He was also a judge at stampedes for many years. His brother, Jim, also married, operated a ranch nearby.

Wed., February 14, 1934. Went to Sigurd Nielsen and got a black bull.[79] Had a terrible time getting him home. Traded Sigurd the wagon box for ten chickens.
February 15, 1934. Was busy getting ready to go to Wayne tomorrow. Bob Kelly was over for his violin lesson. Emmie went over to the Crorys' after supper for the accordion.

The coal mining town of Wayne, north of Hussar, where father peddled chickens, eggs and butter door-to-door, 1930s.

Fri., February 16, 1934. Went to Wayne. Sold eighteen chickens, 7 ½ dozen eggs & twenty lbs. butter. Stopped on way home at Blue Spring School and played for a dance. Got back at 8 a.m. Saturday morning. Started to snow when I left for home.
Sat., February 17, 1934. Didn't go to bed. Was kept busy with chores and violin pupils. Cold weather.
Mon., February 18, 1934. Went to Lawson's, and Phil & I started to halter break the buckskin. Phil Pugh brought the buckskin over today. I left it in the barn. Stormy today. Wrote letter to Alfred.
Wed., February 21, 1934. Made a new table for the kitchen. Syd Petersen [*Emily's brother*] and Shorty [*Westover?*] were over; stopped on their way to Lawson's.

---

[79] Sigurd Nielsen farmed west of my parents. Though so poor in 1934, he was barely surviving, Sigurd would later flourish by hard work and lucky risks—such as investing in a gusher oil well. He became a wealthy man, owning eight or nine sections of land and was later awarded the title of Master Farmer.

Thurs., February 22, 1934. Broke the buckskin, "Tim," to the stoneboat with Pete & Topsy.
Fri., February 23, 1934. Played at Dahl house.
Mon., February 26, 1934. Put the saddle on Tim and rode him for first time. Wrote letter to Dept. of Agriculture about grasshoppers. Warming up.
Fri., March 1 1934. A busy day. Frank Robey came at dinner. Later on Sid Busch came to get a drake. Five of us for supper. I had to hurry to dance at Rabbit lake school dance. Frank went with me. Made $7. Got back at 5:30 a.m.
Sat., March 2, 1934. Frank rode to CX to get his horses. Helped him get them in our field. He picked me out a bronc and roped it in the barn and tied it up.
Sun., March 3, 1934. Frank picked me out another horse (Nigger) and we made the deal, $75 for the two. Paid him $20. He left with his horses at 2 p.m.
Sun., March 11, 1934. The Crory boys brought over the pig they traded with me for violin lessons. George Hayden came over.[80]
Mon., March 12, 1934. Went to Wayne with the buggy. Peddled twenty-five dozen eggs, twenty lbs. butter and eleven chickens.
Tues., March 13, 1934. George & I butchered the pig.
Wed., March 14, 1934. Went over to J.J.'s after a load of oats (forty-five bushels). Stopped at Syd Petersen's to get it ground.
Mon., March 26, 1934. Norman's birthday. Went to Comstock's after two tons of coal and hauled it over to Blakes'.[81] Went by Pontec's and got J.J.'s horse. Got home at 11 p.m.
Wed., March 28, 1934. Cold SE wind. Went to J.J.'s in sleigh with horse. Brought back hay.

In 1934 spring began with heat, wind and dust. With few resources, father tried to harrow his thirty acre stubble field, but there were too many weeds, and he had to resort to discing before seeding into the mulch. He borrowed a horse and bought another old cheap mare, seeding the dried up sloughs with millet and oats. By May 15, he began to poison gophers. It got hot—100 F°.

---

[80] George Hayden, a farm labourer and friend, would later work for us.

[81] Eli ("Babe") and Elizabeth Blake were born in the United States, each emigrating to Canada with their parents. They were married in Lomond, Alberta, in 1921 and moved to the Hawkeye Ranch, north of Hussar. Eventually, they had two farms—one near my parents—and a family of eight children, farming until retirement.

Father and Herb Crory traded machinery, Herb helped father plow, father helped Herb harrow and seed.

On May 23, mother wrote: "Ole was discouraged by the grasshoppers which are hatching by the millions." To combat them, from late autumn 1933 until after harvest 1934, Alberta set up eighty-nine mixing stations to serve 4,500,000 acres, and bait-spreading teams of 15,000 farmers spread 31,637,000 pounds of bait. Father spread his own 1,000 pounds comprised of arsenic mixed with sawdust and bran.[82] *The latter two were for holding water, as the poison was effective only when moist. Father had only to add water to the bait and spread, taking half a day. The occasional shower did not help for long, and by June 23 the grain was drying up. Most of July was very hot and very windy, and there were no wild berries for canning. For a while, father worked at road grading, getting $2.50 a day, then began repairing his binder, which cut badly and constantly broke down. On June 6, he started cutting oats; on June 10, the wheat— finishing all by the next evening, except the oats in the slough.*

Emily and Norman at Petersens', 1934.

By mid-August, dust storms mounted, and my parents began to run out of water for the livestock. One day, after a heavy rain, father tried watering the stock in roadside ditches. These dried up so quickly that two days later mother had to take the animals to the neighbour, Tom Lawson, Sr, who had a perpetual spring. After another dust storm, so bad it blotted out the sun and blasted

[82] Earlier, the bait was Paris Green, later, sodium siloco fluoride—non-poisonous to livestock. James Gray, *Men Against The Desert* (Saskatoon, Sask.: Modern Press, 1967), pp. 39-40.

everything with grit, my parents tried to deepen their own little spring, but the resulting thin trickle meant a return to Lawson's. Then an ungrateful cow broke into the parched garden late that summer and ate most of it.

Father worked on a threshing crew, going from farm to farm, finishing at our place on September 6. "We got 223 bushels from the 30 acres of stubble," noted mother. One more farm was threshed before the outfit broke down. It rained, then snowed and froze hard. It wasn't until October that Crorys got threshed. Father's first load of grain went for 61 cents a bushel for No.1 wheat. At Christmas, over a meal that included æbleskiver*—a Danish tradition—they gathered together and shared the joys of fellowship.*

In all of this, it was probably easier for mother, who did not worry about farming the way father did. As she recorded the events that year, she did so as a matter-of-fact; there was still no alarm in her short notes. As well, she was not far from her parents, her siblings and their families. They got along well, and though all were in a desperate situation, they visited back and forth, helping each other with everything from haircuts to butchering, field work and the use of machinery. At Christmas they gathered at the Petersens', sharing the joys of fellowship.

1935

Day after day, mother wrote of cold weather. On January 12, Norman fell ill, and on the 14th, she took him to Dr. Fletcher at Standard, who advised her to stay at her parents' for a week while Norman was being treated. When father did not come to get them as planned, she rode home on horseback, nineteen miles in the snow, to see why. "Ole was out of coal," she wrote, "and living in the kitchen." Not ill—or she would have mentioned it—it seems he was simply depressed about their situation, in a way which I never knew him to be. All the next day, they thawed and churned the cream he'd stored. The day after that, he drove to the mine for coal. In a few weeks, they were out of feed for their stock. For people then, relief was deeply humiliating, yet father had no choice but to get 150 bushels of relief oats from the government. It took him two days to haul it home. On the second day, he began the following letter:

Chancellor, February 12, 1935
Dear Everyone!

I well realize that you must despair of the long time gone, since last I wrote you a letter. Thank you for the letter sent a long time ago. I am ashamed of myself not answering it then. The only excuse I can find is that it is no fun to write a letter when there is not any good news to report. Many times I have said to myself: To-night I must write home, but when night comes I cannot think of anything that might interest you. But now I can't wait any longer. I'll tell you as best as I can how we live and it's going to be a letter which will make up for some of my silence.

February 17th

It is Sunday afternoon, apologies for the interruption! To continue, last year was a poor year. It was not only the drought, but we suffered with a plague of gophers and grasshoppers. We were forced to put out poison for both. For the gophers, we mix strychnine with grain and put a teaspoonful of poisoned grain in each hole we can find. The poison is quite expensive, and I was not able to buy as much as I would like. For the grasshoppers, we get the poison (arsenic) free from the government. We did not really have very good prospect for a crop this year, as we had no summerfallow last year. I have kept account of my income and expenses [*which I enclose*].

Naturally, you must wonder how we ever make out. We have not dared spend any money for pleasure of any kind, and to tell the truth, the reason I haven't sent you any pictures is the fact that we cannot afford to send an exposed roll away to get it developed and printed. We still insist that we need no further help because we live well and get enough to eat. Everybody in the same neighborhood is in the same fix. And we now have eight horses, nine cows, chickens and nearly all the machinery we need. I have 120 acres of summerfallow ready to seed next year.

Now, this summer, we are going to vote again—both in the Province of Alberta and the Dominion Government. Everything we hear is "Social Credit," a new economical order, and it seems that they will get on top, but I guess that you have read about that.

Account Ledger for 1934

Expenses		Income	
Groceries	$143.33	Wheat sold	$84.30
Threshing	19.00	Butter sold	38.85
Blacksmith	10.35	Eggs sold	16.66
Gasoline	10.72	Horse sold	20.00
Binder twine		Chickens sold	32.30
	5.25	Ducks sold	8.50
Clothes	29.13	Play for dances	39.20
Furniture	34.35	Violin students	23.35
Machinery	26.00	Work wages	
A horse	20.00		46.00
A calf	5.00	Misc.	16.72
Coal	20.00		
Total	**$323.13**	**Total**	**$326.88**

During the year we went into debt for the following:
2 horses..................................... $75.00 (paid $20.00 cash)
Machinery................................. $25.00 (paid $16.00 cash)
Seed oats from Government.... $26.00

Both Norman and Emily are quite well, although both have been a little sick this month, stomach mostly. I'm so happy with Norman; I'll teach him to play the violin when he gets big enough. He doesn't talk much yet, but can say a few words. You can see that the violin (playing and teaching) is helping us quite a bit (over $60). And I believe it will be even better this year. We now have our own dance orchestra here in the neighborhood, and we play for dances in Chancellor, Hussar and others. I often wish that I had father's violin, but I realize that Alfred does not want to see it leave Denmark. I had a radio going for awhile first part of the winter, but the batteries played out, and there were other things we needed worse than radio batteries. For that matter, I have lots to do, and not much spare time. This winter we do not get up quite as early, about 7 a.m., then I milk the cows, feed the horses and cows, while Emily makes breakfast. Should you wonder what we have for breakfast, I can tell you that we eat oatmeal and pancakes. During the summer, we vary the diet with different egg dishes, once in awhile. We eat dinner at 12 o'clock and supper at 6 p.m. During the day, there is always work for me to do outside.

After supper I milk the cows once again and feed the stock. We go to bed between 9 and 10 o'clock on weekdays. On Thursdays my students come, and on Saturdays I ride a horse to a schoolhouse where I meet a couple of students that have too long a distance to come to our farm. Other times I go to practices with our orchestra. Once in a while, Emily and Norman go with me. On Sundays we often have visitors, or we go to visit somewhere.

Simple Life? Right? But it is not always that way. From Christmas until the end of January, it was bitterly cold, the worst cold we have had for many years, from 10 below to 42 below Fahrenheit. To go any place we must be well wrapped up. Many days there is a strong bitterly cold wind that sometimes blows itself into a blizzard, and then it is impossible to do much of anything outside. We burned over two tons of coal in three weeks, and even then we could hardly keep warm. I have an alarm clock which I set to ring twice during the night so I can get up and put more coal in the heater. Then all of a sudden one night the temperature went from 10 below to 44 above, and we have had nice weather since. I had never dreamt that times could get so tough. Had I known, I might have changed my mind about farming, but now I have too much invested, and I do believe that times are getting somewhat better.

My Danish is not very good, I'm afraid. I think you will find some mistakes in this letter, and I have tried so hard to make this a good Danish letter. I don't see enough Danes, and those I speak to all use half and half. Only a person who knows both languages could figure it out.

With lots of love to you all, again, thank you for still thinking of us.

Emily and Helge

P. S. I will write a little letter to the girls [*Alfred and Gudrun's daughters*].

Though father's first days at discing began with a dust storm so fierce that he had to quit in the fields, and though he was feeding his horses with Petersen oats and seeding with Petersen wheat, the month of May 1935, was promising—mostly fair or cool with days of rain and showers.

But by mid-June they were getting extremely hot weather. Any rain that fell evaporated before it hit the soil, or soon thereafter. Sometimes it immediately formed a hard crust on the earth, repelling the water. On the hill tops, the grain had mostly dried out or blown away, and in the low-lying areas, it stood wilting in the rippling heat, when on July 6th, the *skies cracked open. The violent cloudburst spared them, but mother's brother, Sydney, and sister, Vera, were completely hailed out. Petersens lost their oats to hail in August.*

Clayton Crory worked for us that summer. Father bought an old binder from Jim Lawson for $25, and sold the old Ford for $10 and twelve hens.

Ole on binder, 1935. On the back, Ole wrote to Alfred and Gudrun, "I suppose you have seen these kinds of pictures often. You can see the grain is thin on the hills."

1936

During January and February, mother talked of bitterly cold weather. In April, after cleaning his grain, father poisoned gophers and took 106 bushels of oats over to the Petersens, who had lost theirs to hail the year before. Father and Bob Kelly went to a Social Credit meeting, and on August 25, he, mother and Lulu English, hired during harvest, voted for Social Credit.[83]

That year, as usual, mother sewed most of Norman's and her clothes, baked bread, hand-churned 117 pounds of butter—much of it for sale—canned 48 quarts of beef, preserved a butchered pig by soaking it in brine,

[83] Lulu, born in Idaho, moved to Canada in 1917 with her parents, Tom and Cora, and six siblings. They rented a farm in the Wintering Hills, but when some of the children were quite small, Tom died. "Blondie," as she was known, was a good cook and hard worker, and had many friends, among them, my parents.

and preserved pork, ham and sausages. She also canned 16 quarts of currants; 2 quarts and 1 pint of jelly; 50 quarts and 24 pints of vegetables; 35 quarts of chokecherry jelly; and 22 quarts of fruit, from her garden. Besides the usual carrots, cabbage, etc., they stored 71 four-gallon pails of potatoes. From her poultry (not counting the seldom-noted sale of eggs) they made about $140 cash—much of this from dressed ducks and geese sold in Hussar and Wayne. As well, she helped out in every way possible with day-to-day farm operations while caring for young Norman and being pregnant most of the year.

Hussar, February 6, 1936
Dear Gudrun and Alfred!

Thank you for the X-mas letter. I received it just before X-mas; it was full of good news. I wish I could think of as much to tell you about, then I would write more often. I don't feel that my ordinary life can be of any interest to you, way over in Denmark, and we have not got far enough ahead to take advantage of our beautiful Alberta scenery so we can describe our tours and send you pictures. There is one thing that I always hold fast to, and that is the fact that Alfred was my foster father in Denmark, and in my thoughts you will always remain so. Here in Alberta, although I'm married to a good girl who has wonderful parents, there are still many times I'm more or less a "Stranger" in my thoughts. And many times I ask myself, what would Alfred advise me to do in such a case? I guess it must be a "hold-over" from days of old. It's not that I'm afraid to stand on my own two legs, but I guess it's only natural to have a mentor. So remember, Alfred, that when I write you and ask you about something, it doesn't matter if you think you're not able to give me a good answer since you are so far away. It is my foster father who is being asked—I don't have one of those over here.

I'm enclosing a slip of paper showing my cash account for 1935. It contains larger figures than for 1934, but the net result is the same. Still, we have made some progress. Last year I borrowed seed wheat from father-in-law; that I have returned, and I have kept 275 bushels of seed wheat for 1936. I have 300 bushels of oats in a granary. We have also traded around and now have three pigs. It is my first endeavour in hogs, but they are in fair price now, and do not cost as much to feed. Last year I had only 125 acres in crop; this year I'll have 190 acres summerfallow, along with 50 acres stubble (soil which has been seeded once since it was plowed) to seed. Besides this I have rented 130 acres summerfallow from a land company in Calgary. I was lucky enough to get a contract where I get to keep three-quarters of the grain instead of the usual two-thirds. Our cows are growing in size as well as numbers. We now have a bull, six cows and four heifers. It is no wonder that they are not sold, because the price of cattle is very poor. We have 160 acres of grassland, which doesn't cost us anything. So you can surely see that we are getting along and progressing, even if our pockets are empty. We are not hysterical about that because it was like that last year and the year before. We still have butter and eggs for sale, and if needed, we can get a little credit. Later in the summer, we have chickens to sell, and if we have to, we can always sell a cow or calf.

Account Ledger for 1935

Expenses

Groceries	$105	Dentist	10.00
Coal	18.30	Misc.	54.12
Small things for household	10.27	100 bus. wheat for Petersen	68.00
Glass jars for fruit preserves	9.95	Threshing	141.64
Clothes	98.32	Twine for Self Binder	23.00
Horses	40.80	Trucking grain to elevator	27.00
Blacksmith	2.30	Radio	60.00
Fuel for light	6.95	Machinery, harness repair, etc.	31.30
Gas for pump (water for stock)	4.25	Expenses in Calgary, etc.	0.35
Oyster shells for hens	3.15	Tobacco	8.75
Gopher poison	3.25	**Total**	**776.20**
Medicine	9.50		

Income

Wheat	$547.14	Violin lessons	10.50
Butter	50.60	[Playing for] Dances	38.25
Eggs	26.11	Meals, threshers	36.00
Potatoes	6.10	Misc.	29.20
Chickens	35.00	**Total**	**778.90**

Actually, it looks pretty good for us, as long as we can keep our health. That is my biggest worry now. We are healthy now, but I can't help wondering how long we must be scraping the bottom of the barrel? One thing is for sure, I have a wonderful wife who has taught me where we can save in so many things. If anybody will manage, we will.

On March 26th, Norman will be three years old. He has to imitate every thing I do. He doesn't talk much yet. This is likely because Emily is so hard-of-hearing. It is over half a year since he could say, "Daddy," "Mamma," etc. I'm sure he could learn to talk much faster, but instead of asking his mother about something, he takes her by the hand and shows her what he wants. I thought sure that through the winter when I was in the house I could get him started talking, but I haven't got very far yet. I've tried to make him say something, and usually he won't even try. Other people advise us not to worry about it—he will be talking when he is ready, but he is so smart in all other ways. There are, of course, no other children he can play with. Another thing, he has not yet been baptized; it will have to wait until next fall. So we all have our own little trials, but we are healthy and happy in our little family.

I send you many loving greetings from all three of us,

Helge

NB! You will see that I have addressed this letter from Hussar. We have found that we do better business in Hussar, and it's one mile closer than Chancellor. Should a letter come, addressed to Chancellor, it will go to Hussar, so no harm will be done.

P.S. You sent us a very good picture of Paarup County. I tried to find the old places I remembered but was not able to figure it out. Emily often asks about Denmark. I wonder, could you send us a little map of Denmark so I can explain the Danish geography to her?

The year 1936 had been bone dry in Alberta. Under ten inches of rain fell at Calgary and Medicine Hat, and parts between the two cities were drier still. All summer the crops scorched in the hot sun—even the berry patch was devoid of saskatoons. Mother wrote in July, "Our grain was drying up and things do really look bad for us." Their harvest on summerfallow wheat went 6.3 bushels to the acre, and they did not even cut their stubble wheat.[84] *By December 5, it turned so cold they nearly*

[84] The summerfallow produced more grain because, lying fallow for a year, it had collected more moisture than the stubble field which had grown a crop the year before.

froze in their beds. That month they killed and dressed forty-six ducks and thirteen geese, which father sold at Wayne and Hussar.

Ole and Norman with Queenie and her pups. Beyond, the parched fields and pasture, summer 1936.

1937

During the last few weeks of her confinement, mother stayed at the Petersens, and on January 15, I was born. The next day, mother didn't feel well. After supper on the 17th, she became very ill, with a high fever, and on the 23rd she was driven to Calgary, so sick that it was March 17 before she was allowed to sit up for a few minutes.

Hussar, March 6, 1937
Dear Gudrun and Alfred!

I have waited for some time before writing a letter, hoping that I would have some good news. Life can deal you some awful hard blows sometime. The day after I sent you my enthusiastic letter about the birth of little Joan, I received a telephone call that Emily was very seriously sick, and for me to hurry to Standard. When I got there [*at Lee's Nursing Home*] I couldn't believe my own eyes. She was so thin and pale. The doctor admitted that he was afraid she had blood poison and that he was afraid that she may not survive the ordeal. She has had a very high temperature for several days, and the day after I saw her, the temperature went way down below normal, and it was his opinion that her system had given up the fight.

Of course, I asked him if it would be better to send her to Calgary, where they have several large hospitals and many outstanding doctors. He was afraid that she could not stand the sixty-five mile trip to the city in a car, and the train was much too slow. However, he had heard of a new wonder drug [*probably Sulfa drugs, in use for about two years*] that might save her life. He phoned to Calgary to find out if it was available there. Getting the affirmative answer, my two brothers-in-law [*Herman and Walter*] jumped in a car and raced for Calgary at 4:30 in the morning. They came back by 7 o'clock, and the doctor administered the drug at once. During the day, she showed some improvements, and on the doctor's advice she was sent by ambulance to Calgary, more dead than alive. I stayed in Calgary for two weeks, the worst two weeks I've ever experienced! I could not get a word out of her two doctors, except that she was seriously ill. Finally, the day came when they could say that she had a good chance to survive and that I could go back to the farm again, because they estimated it would take about three months before she could come home. She was in a private room that cost $5.25 a day. But, after three weeks, she felt good enough to move into a ward with three other patients ($2.75 per day).

She is still there, and it is hard to know how long she must stay. So all our plans and money have vanished into thin air. But if she recovers in good shape, we will just have to start all over again. Our little daughter is still in the nursing home at Standard. I drive in to see her once in awhile. Norman stays with his grandparents, and I have a man helping me out here on the farm so that I can get away once in a while. Now, as to Emily's sickness, I asked the doctor in Calgary before I left. He did not think it was a genuine case of blood poison—he called it an inflammation of the pelvis and uterus. Emily had a large lump on her left side. The severest of her pains left after she had been in the hospital two weeks. She has had no operation, and not very much medicine. The doctors are trying to just assist her own system to fight her illness. She was not allowed to lie down flat for over a month and she gets so tired, sitting up in her bed, trying to get some sleep. I phone her every second day, and write as often as I can. It will take us a long, long time to pay up our debt to the doctors and the hospital, but it will be worth it, if she can be her own self again. She is so lonesome for her little daughter.

I myself have been sick with stomach flu the last week or so. While batching I have learned to churn butter, wash clothes, iron and cook. I try to have things look like they do when she is home. When Emily finally can get out of the hospital, she will have to stay with her parents for a month or so, until she gets strong enough to come back to our farm. I hate to write this kind of letter to you, but I think it would be wrong to let you believe that everything is so wonderful (which, in my last letter, I led you to believe).

I look forward to the day when I will have my whole little family with me again. I hope that you are all well and that God will save you from sickness and sadness. Lots of love to all five of you and others of the family.

Helge

On March 20, father drove mother from Calgary to her parents' farm to convalesce, taking five hours—they kept getting stuck in drifts. A couple of weeks later, the Petersens brought me, in failing health, from the nursing home, and I joined Mother and Norman. There we were well cared for, especially by Isobel Michie, Herman's girl friend, now working at the Petersens'.

This, the last of father's letters, was written on brown wrapping paper:

[*Hussar*] May 6, 1937
Dear Gudrun and Alfred!

Many thanks for your letter, dated April 9th. I received it last Saturday. I have been so busy with spring work that I will not be able to go to the Post Office until next Saturday; and thank you for the money—it was indeed welcome! I shall remember your generosity, and I hope the day will soon come when I can repay you. Your money gave me some relief from the bills piling up on me. The hospital and the doctor gave me credit until such time when I'll be able to pay up my bills. We have had a very poor harvest, and besides, we have had to hire a girl to help Emily with the housework. The doctor told us that the money we spend on a girl will be recovered in fewer trips to the hospital for Emily, and fewer bills from the doctors. She is now slowly recovering. She is already talking about letting the girl go, as we cannot afford it, but I won't hear of it.

Emily and I are intending to move away from this farm when Norman reaches school age, as there are over five miles to the nearest school, and that is too far for a little boy, especially in the cold winter time. We would move right away if we had a good enough outfit, which we do not have. We have been waiting for a good harvest so we can buy a tractor and machinery. We have been hanging on to our stock in hope of finding a place with better pastures, and next summer I intend to go looking for it. There are much better places here in Alberta, if we could only get on our feet again.

Ole with eight horse team, Hussar, 1937.

The last three days, I have been working the land with a seven horse team, in such a dust storm that I could see nothing further away than ten meters (thirty feet). It is late now, and I'm dead tired, so more about the future in my next letter. Little Joan is growing like a weed, and we love her dearly, though she arrived under very tragic circumstances.

Most of the questions in your letter were answered in my last letter. I must say, you were prompt and even mailed it by airmail. Again my heartfelt thanks. As I told you, I'm seeding only 130 acres of summerfallow with wheat. I had to cultivate the ground before I could seed the wheat. I have almost no feed for the horses. I get up at 4:30 in the morning, milk four cows (soon six), make a fire in the house, wake up the girl, ride out in the pasture after the horses, throw the harness on them, eat my breakfast and work the horses for as long as they can last. My supper is at 7 o'clock, then I ride to the pasture after the cows, milk them, separate the milk and get to bed by 10:30. So now I'll say good night, and God bless you all.

Sincerely Yours,

Helge

In mid-April, when father brought us home to our farm, it was the first time mother and Norman had been together since New Year's. In May mother went back to Calgary for a week of reparative surgery. The hospital bills piled up, with neither medical insurance nor money to pay them.

By June 3rd, even mother was worried: "It was blowing all day & nearly all our crops blew out. It sure looked bad for us." A "nice little shower" in the first week of July was not enough to revive the remaining grain, and soon she wrote that the weather was "awful hot and our crop was nearly all gone." A heavy rain across the prairies in mid-July saved us from total disaster, but caused Russian Thistle seeds, dormant for half a decade, to burst forth into a carpet of green at our place and on millions of acres in Alberta and Saskatchewan. For nine days in August, father cut and stacked Russian thistle, getting seventeen hayracks full, poor quality green feed, but providing some nourishment and roughage.

Emily and Joan at Petersens', 1937.

Our harvest brought 650 bushels of wheat, at least some of it #3 grade, and 350 bushels of oats. At Hussar we got four boxes of relief apples.

Oadland's outfit threshing Nissens' frozen wheat. Left, Mike Christensen, Hussar, Oct. 22, 1937.

1938

Around us the drought and Depression were taking a terrible toll. Maybe that explains the strange, sad case of my parents' neighbour, known as Fagert—no one remembers his first name. Fagert had had quite a good threshing outfit in the early 1920s. Now other neighbours noted that he prowled the countryside with a gunnysack on his back, and that things such as tools disappeared in his passing. Though mother disliked him, he started coming to our place, occasionally, in early 1938, for milk and meals. Once he loaned us his fanning mill. Around then Clarence Harmer, who lived nearby, noticed that his horses were getting slower and slower and that he was having a hard time getting his fieldwork done. It turned out that after he had put them in his pasture at night, Fagert took them out and used them to work his own land. In early January 1939, Fagert was jailed for five months when the RCMP caught him with the head of one of Willard Treacy's calves in his oven.

Obviously, survival was easiest for farmers who were debt-free at the onset of the Depression. They hung on, trying everything they could to stretch their meager incomes. Others just dug in and waited. For still others, foreclosure or defeat loomed, and some just walked away from their farms, leaving everything. In the Depression years, a quarter of a million people farming in the Palliser Triangle packed up and moved away—as was happening around us. The Bob Halsey family left sometime in the 1930s. In 1931, Frank Burns left, and at Dorothy, Russell Kidd lost his store. (Twelve years later, Elmer Currie, whose farm *was burned in the prairie fire in 1929, found Kidd at Drumheller, after a long search, and paid an accrued grocery bill). The "Shorty" Westovers left in 1932. The T. Larsens put their land up for sale and moved to Viking in 1937, the same year that the Ed Harpers left. In 1938, there was a farewell party for neighbours by the name of Solis; the Clarence Harmers moved to Calgary and Herb Croughs, to Millet, Alberta. The Croughs later sold their land for $5 an acre, taking years to get paid. In 1939, the Mckinneys returned to Washington, after inheriting land there.*

In June, mother's brother, Sydney, and family called it quits, leaving for Crammond, near Caroline. Father went along to help. At Hussar, the next day, there was a very bad dust storm, and the day after that, the worst one of the year. When father returned, he had to re-seed the blown-out oats.

Sydney and Clara (Busch) Petersen—Emily Nissen's brother and sister-in-law—left the prairies in 1938. Crammond, Alberta, c 1941.

Then mother's sister, Vera Elliott, and her family left for the Garrington district, east of Crammond. They had just lost a partnership in the famous Two Bar Ranch that Jack Morton had once owned, and also lost. Ernie, Vera's husband, drove a four-horse team that pulled their hayrack loaded with all their household goods with a tarp across one corner for shelter for three of their children. Their ten-year-old boy drove a team, pulling a grain tank with the chickens, pigs and grain. Vera brought up the rear, riding a saddle horse, herding sixty horses and about twenty head of cattle. Later, Father loaded his haying outfit onto the hayrack and again travelled to Crammond, where he worked for almost a month.

For Emily's parents, this was not a happy occasion, for another of their children's families was leaving. Back row, George Hayden (friend, hired man) Herman Petersen, Jesse (J.J.) Petersen, Mike Christensen, Mary Petersen, Norman and Ole Nissen. Seated on grass, Isobel Michie, Herman's girl friend and later wife, holding Joan Nissen. Emily took this photo. Standard, July 1938.

Ole and Emily Nissen, camping while looking for another farm west of Calgary, July 1938.

My parents, who wanted to move closer to a school, were now at a pivotal time in their lives, deciding whether to leave the prairies or lease another farm around Standard or Hussar—and there were plenty farms for lease. They must have turned this question over many times in their minds. And it is so ironic that after years of struggle and hardship, they made the wrong decision.

Mother mended the holes in their tent, father fixed their old Ford, and they went searching for another farm further west and north.[85] *Unsuccessful but still determined, they returned, and not even after their best harvest ever—1,200 bushels of wheat and 1,401 bushels of oats in 1938—did they realize that the severe drought was over, and that there good years ahead for prairie farmers, many with bumper crops. In November father found a farm about a mile from Sydney Petersen's, near Crammond, south of Caroline. After years of prairie drought, the bush country, so lush with its fragrant spruce and pine, its wild flowers and blueberries, was tempting. All during the drought, people had moved here, but the best places were gone, and the farm that father chose was not fully productive. Some land needed breaking, the pasture needed fencing, and the old house turned out to have bedbugs—hard to eradicate from between the logs.*

We stayed at the Hussar farm until the next spring, when with George Hayden's help, my folks got ready to move. Machinery was dismantled, fences rolled up, crates built, ropes made. Rosie, the cow, was sold, and horses were traded for a better team. Neighbours came over with a large Pyrex bowl as a farewell gift. Then, without the Free Rate, as in 1932, our belongings were loaded onto trucks, and on April 13, we drove away.

On our departure, Herman removed the windows from our tarpaper shack, and it became another abandoned prairie home.

[85] On their way, my parents visited Walter Schang, still living near Shepard. His home overlooked that of a widow, Pauline Pearson, with two daughters, living in the valley below. Pauline regularly rode with Walter to town for shopping. The two were becoming friends, and would marry and have a son, Gary. They would farm until 1960, then operate a motel in Calgary. Walter died in 1964 at the age of sixty-nine.

EPILOGUE
"I've Had A Good Life"
1939 - 1979

Ole Nissen, 1973

At Crammond, in 1939, my parents began to build a place of their own. Father put in a small crop, fenced, cut brush, pulled stumps, and broke new land. In the fall, he felled trees, had them milled, and within a year and a half—with help from Sydney Petersen and neighbours—built a small home. Besides her other chores, mother built kitchen cupboards, carved a wooden sink, made a drop leaf table, and sewed us all clothes. She burned brush, planted twenty-six fruit trees, shingled the roofs, filled the cracks of the log buildings, and picked and sold hundreds of pounds of blueberries. Some evenings, when the work was done and we children were in bed, my parents would sit outside, in front of their new house. Dad would play the violin, and mother would put on her hearing aid and listen.

To mother it was a rich and fulfilling life. She made a quilt called "Road to Fortune," father played in Pinky Pitt's and Lamb's orchestras, and they had a calf called Hope, a newly broken pony called Slowdown and a mean (formerly stray) dog called Hitler.

But mother was often ill, and no matter how hard they tried, they kept "scraping the bottom of the barrel." Within three years, she was hospitalized for a total of thirty-nine days. In the first autumn, she was critically ill with appendicitis, and though father could not pay, the doctor operated anyway. In the next two years, she had had three more operations and learned from another specialist that Dr. Spankie, her ear and nose doctor since 1930, "had not treated her ear right" —it was too late for a mastoid operation, and she would always need her hearing-aid.

The harvests were small—in 1940, 412 bushels of oats, 145 bushels of wheat; the next year, after days of frost and snow, 488 bushels of oats, 49 bushels of wheat and 398 bundles of green feed. The year 1942 promised no better. By July 30, it had rained almost every day when, without previous discussion, father announced that he had had enough of farming. He began training as an Alberta Wheat Pool agent at Ponoka, and Mother did as so many others had done those years—with shattered dreams—subleased the farm and began selling and giving away the animals and machinery, including her favorite pony. Midway, she again fell ill, but doctors in Calgary could find nothing wrong.

Ole Nissen at the Alberta Wheat Pool elevator with George Hayden, friend from the prairies, McLaughlin, Alberta, c 1944.

Father's first position was at McLaughlin, Alberta—population about eighty. Integration took time, as father found that buying grain had its problems, too. He lost at least one major customer, and had other setbacks which he took hard. Norman had trouble relating with the town kids, and I was forever into mischief. With no more setting hens to keep track of, nor dates of seeding or threshing, mother quit her diary, not long after noting, "There isn't much to write [*about*], it just rains and rains."

The adjustment was hardest for her—for laborious as the work was, farming and all it entailed had been an integral part of her nature. She had been born on a farm, had loved the animals and prairies, and now she missed them. There, also, her hearing impairment had been less of a problem. But mostly, her contribution in labour and planning had been extremely important, and being the wife of a salaried worker did not compare.

Along with this was a terrible undercurrent—as with many other Canadians—the worry about loved ones in Europe. Denmark was invaded by Germany, but remained neutral in those perilous times. Radio news was closely followed; Matthew Halton of the BBC was heard. Maps were studied, parcels were made and sent after being packed and repacked many times till the coffee, dates, and chocolate, etc., formed a solid block. Communication from Denmark was rare, and only by a Red Cross letter did we learn that all father's people had been spared.

In McLaughlin by 1944, things had improved for us. My parents made long-lasting friendships, many with farmers. With father's rural experience and improved business skills, he did well, and no matter what the weather, they enjoyed a steady income and paid their bills. Father played for local dances in what became known, unofficially, as "Ole's orchestra." And, finally, at war's end, with greatest joy, even this little community had its victory parade, with a piper, drums and flags.

We left McLaughlin around 1952. The community held a farewell dance, with the proceeds a gift. At the end of the evening, the large crowd ringing the hall, sang "For They are Jolly Good Fellows," with the four of us in the centre, father abashedly pleased.

Father had been offered a transfer to Irma, Alberta, operating double Pool elevators. This move was happier. The village with a population of about 450, was an exciting prospect. As before, my father's music helped us integrate. Many evenings, in rural homes filled with music and laughter, father practised with the orchestra. Mother visited, while we children slept upstairs with farm friends.

Father was involved in many town activities. He was on the town council, in the Elks, 4-H Clubs, and the Masonic Lodge (becoming Grand Steward). He organized amateur theatre, played for dances, weddings, etc., and took part in sports days, fiddling contests (which he usually won), and curling. He had great staying-power. He could work extremely hard all day—shovelling damp grain, moving great, heavy, railway cars into place with a hand-jack, and papering the insides and filling them. Then he would play for a dance until two or three in the morning.

Unfortunately, he continued to worry. Whether this was a tendency brought on by the Depression years, or whether it was just his nature, cannot be known. In 1952 he had an operation for stomach ulcers, then thought to be caused by stress. He was partly successful in his resolve to take things easier.

Father's gregariousness, though, was a boon, and among his friends were other grain-buyers. At McLaughlin, Eric Collins, of Alberta Pacific Grain, said, "We never let competition interfere with our friendship." He and father would get their holidays in August, rent a cabin, and, with their families, go fishing. At Irma, in retirement, father and Charlie Milne, the former United Grain

Ole and Emily Nissen, on their 25th anniversary, April 1956.

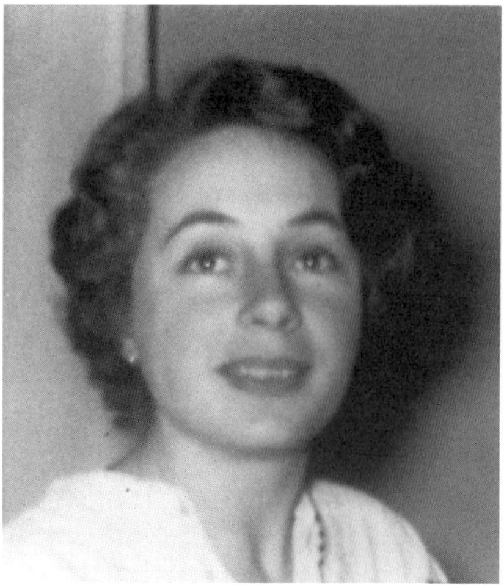

The Nissen children, Norman Nissen, 1952, and Joan Walter, 1961.

Growers' buyer, competed with their gardens. "Wait'll Charlie sees this!" Dad once said, tying huge store-bought tomatoes onto his garden plants. Father liked home movies, one of which was a double exposure showing a large Christmas gathering of neighbours in our living room, laughing and smiling as father in his boat sailed through, holding up his fish for admiration.

At times father would mention the farm, saying that he should have bought a tractor instead of using horses, and that 1942, with rising produce prices, was a bad time to quit. But I don't think he ever regretted his decision. He made it and never looked back. Mother's medical bills were a part of their failure, but they weren't her fault, and father never made her feel bad about it. Neither did mother blame him for giving up.

Though, in ways, mother never stopped missing the farm, she adapted. At Irma, she grew a large garden, raised chickens and rabbits, and kept a spotless and attractive home. These were good times for us all—until 1954 when mother became ill with cancer. I cared for her that last fall, injecting her with painkillers as she displayed the same courage that had sustained her in the Depression years. She died in 1956, at the age of forty-eight.

In 1958 father married Audrey Jones of Irma, who played piano with the local orchestra. They had a son and a daughter who are now both married, each with two children of their own, residing at, or near Irma. Eric works for Northwestern Utilities and is on the town council, Fay and her husband, Kelly Overbo, have a construction business. Both Fay and Eric's wife, Debra, work

Ole and Audrey Nissen at a 4-H convention, Olds, Alberta.

outside the home. Norman became a plumber and pipe fitter, working most of his life in Alberta. He remains a bachelor, is retired, and lives in Toronto. I married a fellow student, Art Walter, whom I met while studying visual arts, the field in which we have made a living. We reside in Winnipeg. Four children were born to us, and we have four grandchildren.

Ole and Audrey Nissen's children, Eric Nissen, 1986, and Fay Overbo, c 1991.

In Denmark, Ole photographed his siblings: Vilhelm, Eijner, Alfred, Lex, Johannes, Ingrid, on the ship which Vilhelm captained. Nykøbing, Falster, 1952.

In 1952, father's siblings combined funds so that he could visit them in Denmark—the first time since he'd left twenty-nine years before. (Mother, not well, stayed home.) It was a momentous occasion for him to see them all again, but sad to part. Later, he took several more trips, one to celebrate Alfred and Gudrun's Golden Wedding Anniversary. In English and halting Danish, father gave a moving speech in appreciation of their many years of love and guidance. Gudrun died in 1969, Alfred, in 1972.

At Standard, the Petersen farmily is now owned and operated by the university-educated third generation. One day I learned from my cousin, Dean Petersen, what it means to have a sense of place. Standing on a high hill overlooking the farm, with the countryside and mountains beyond, he pointed out the homes of his parents, brother, sister, and their families, and his uncles, friends and neighbours—there was the whole community in an area where the Petersens have lived since 1910.

At my parents' former farm, north of Hussar, now owned by Art and Dianne Taubert, all that remain are signs of a well, a few bits of pottery and a hawthorn tree.

Father retired from the Pool at age sixty-five, enthusiastically taking on two more jobs, as accountant for the Co-op store, and as an insurance agent in a business he had established—later run by Audrey. Theirs was a happy, bustling household, where Norman and I, friends and family, were always welcome. They had twenty-one good years together.

Father died in 1979, at the age of seventy-five. He and a cousin from Denmark had been boating on a northern Alberta lake, singing Danish songs in the setting sun, their laughter echoing across the water. On reaching shore, father pulled up the boat, lit a cigarette and suffered a massive heart attack. For his funeral, the Irma United Church, though recently enlarged, was too small—it had to be held in the school auditorium.

At the Irma Cemetery, as his Masonic brothers filed past his grave, each placing on it a bough of evergreen, I remembered how, only a week or so before, father had tried to prepare me for his death. "I don't want you feeling bad about it," he had said. "I'm getting older and more tired. I've had a good life, and when the time comes, I'll be ready."

Appendix

Average Annual Prices of Number 1 Northern Wheat, Canada, 1906 to 1945
(Prices in cents)

1906	78.8	1919	217.4	1933	68.1
1907	105.2	1920	199.4	1934	81/7
1908	109.0	1921	129.7	1935	85/1
1909	101.1	1922	110.5	1936	122/5
1910	94.2	1923	107.0	1937	131/4
1911	100.8	1924	168.5	1938	62/0
1912	90.1	1925	151.2	1939	76/4
1913	89.1	1926	146.2	1940	74/0
1914	132.4	1927	146.3	1941	76/5
1915	113.6	1928	124.0	1942	94/4
1916	205.5	1929	124.2	1943	123/2
1917	221.1	1930	64.2	1944	125/0
1918	224.2	1931	59.8	1945	125/0
		1932	54.3		

Source: F.H. Leacy, *Historical Statistics of Canada* (Ottawa: Statistics Canada & Social Science Federation of Canada, 1983), np. Fractions are in tenths of a cent until 1933, then in eights.

In this period, in the Hussar area, a "good wheat crop" yielded 20 to 30 bushels an acre; a "bumper crop,"35 to 50 bushels.

INDEX